T0290531

Constant Berkhout

THE RETAIL INNOVATION TOOLKIT

42 CATEGORY MANAGEMENT TOOLS FOR GROWTH

Lannoo
Campus

To Carola, Thomas and Isabel,
with whom I learn, unlearn
and relearn every day

Every reasonable attempt has been made to identify owners of copyright.
Any errors or omissions brought to the publisher's attention will be
corrected in subsequent editions.

D/2021/45/192 – ISBN 978 94 014 7719 2 – NUR 800

Cover and interior design: Wendy De Haes

© Constant Berkhout & Lannoo Publishers nv, Tielt, 2021.

LannooCampus Publishers is a subsidiary of Lannoo Publishers,
the book and multimedia division of Lannoo Publishers nv.

LannooCampus Publishers
Vaartkom 41 box 01.02   P.O. Box 23202
3000 Leuven   1100 DS Amsterdam
Belgium   Netherlands
www.lannoocampus.com

Contents

THE RETAIL INNOVATION TOOLKIT

3 Build Category Assortment   75

4 Deliver Smart Pricing and Promotion   101

5 Leverage Category in Supplier – Retailer Relationship   127

Introduction

Welcome!

Over the last couple of years, the world of retail has experienced a massive disruption as a result of the increasing share of online sales, digitisation of services, rise of discount brands, higher competitive pressure driven by decreasing population growth, and consumer demand for sustainable, transparent solutions. These developments require a new perspective on shopping, and perhaps even a reinvention of current retail models. To mobilise change, organisations do not only need a clear vision from top management but also fresh perspectives from all team members and partners across the value chain. This book offers tools to help retailers and their suppliers to analyse, activate and innovate their categories, and to improve mutual collaboration.

Retailer: Desire to connect with the shopper

Shopping at a retailer where you are known and where your personal needs are met feels so much better. Shoppers experience that service best in mom-and-pop stores, but this retail model has become hard to operate and make profitable today. Though retailers are still in direct contact with their customers, they have not been able to maintain that level of personalisation. For many years, the best shoppers got were pictures of friendly smiling staff at the entrance and statements about customer-driven values chalked on the wall. Fortunately, digitisation of retail operations and data analytics allow retailers to reestablish this personal connection with the shopper. There is not much time to lose because shoppers easily get used to new services and increase their expectations each time someone in the marketplace improves the shopping experience. Shoppers have come to expect the best 24/7 service and the highest quality at the lowest possible price. Oh, and don't forget to make the retail business fully transparent with regard to costs, fair labour practices, impact on the planet and supplier business practices. The sudden rise of COVID-19 has come as a wake-up call for new approaches to product delivery logistics and store operations. However, the need for change was already there.

Supplier: New ways of bonding with the shopper

When suppliers take an optimistic view on the current Cambrian diversification of media and distribution channels, they see more touchpoints to start and build their relationships with shoppers. In fact, media and distribution are merging as illustrated by the combination of Google Search and Shopping, the buy buttons on social media such as Instagram, and the digital advertising screens in brick-and-mortar stores. Historic definitions of what channels are disappear as retailers continuously add new categories in search of incremental revenue. They come up with new, seemingly weird combinations such as books and eye care, and a hairdresser with a bicycle shop. Every time a new type of retail model arrives on the scene, such as category killers, TV-shopping and service-oriented hard discount, suppliers need to assess if they match their brands. New business models such as market places, search engines and comparison websites create the possibility to deliver the shopper directly and restrict the number of intermediary players. We always assumed that categories such as shoes and fresh produce required personal assistance till Zappos and Ocado taught us that shoppers enjoy buying these online. It is no longer sufficient to ask shoppers for feedback on the product itself, because shoppers evaluate the full shopping journey from search till consumption. It's not just the product, but also the characteristics of the context that make the brand. The old days of imposing the consumer price and the control on brand experience are not coming back. The diversification of media and distribution channels offer suppliers great starting points for co-creation with retailers and shoppers.

Meeting point: Category level

It's not just a matter of technology. The world is changing at such high speed that people across functions and organisations need to mobilise and acquire the right set of innovation competencies. Retailers and suppliers need to prepare their own organisations, but also seek ways of working together. The natural level of conversation between the two is the category, because the category level allows space for discussion where the interests of retailers (coming from the perspective of the complete store and retail brand) and those of suppliers (coming from their brands' perspective) meet and can be taken to new heights. Category management can be defined as a retailer-supplier process of managing categories as business units with the goal of delivering consumer value.[1] This may seem a bit abstract and it helps to realise that the category management philosophy rests on a number of core principles: think category rather than brand or product segment level, deliver value to consumers, enhance collaboration between retailer and supplier, and consider the interaction between supply and demand activities. The creation of sustainable value for consumers by building on the mutual interests of retailers and suppliers offers great inspiration for addressing today's challenges. Since the birth of category management some 25 years ago, the world has changed. Thus, while keeping the mindset and positive aspects of category management, new category management working practices need to be embraced:

- Complement the consumer focus with shopper experiences;
- Shift from project to process way of working;
- Apply advanced analytical tools to explore new data opportunities;
- Be versatile across formats, channels, markets.

The Retail Innovation Toolkit

I obtained the ideas for this book when working in the fields of Category Management, Customer Experience, Product Innovation and Design Thinking. Just as the world of retail is mixing things, combining ideas from these different fields helps retailers and suppliers to learn and implement new ways of meeting the (future) expectations of shoppers. The tools in this book help you to analyse, grow, innovate and even reinvent categories in a quick and an enjoyable manner. To facilitate the application in your working environment, I kept the text short and focused. Therefore, the step-by-step instructions are enriched with visualisations of the tools and case studies across a high number of industries. The toolkit offers both basic tools and more complex exercises. Each of the tools indicates the expected experience level, the ideal number of participants and the duration of the action phase. Together they constitute a great manual and reference book to help professionals on both the retail and supply sides accelerate their

---

1   Definition based on: Category Management Best Practices Report, ECR Europe (1997).

understanding and skills of managing categories and improving trade relationships. In summary, the rationale of the book is:

- Today's retail landscape is changing rapidly and dramatically.
- The category is a great meeting point for building partnerships.
- Combining techniques from category management and other fields builds a skillset on how to analyse and activate categories.
- The design of the book allows you to read with a goal in mind and to absorb lots of information at a time.

Who could benefit from the book?

The toolkit is developed for professionals working in shopper and trade marketing on the supplier side, and for category managers, format managers and concept developers in (non)food retail. The tools also enable other functions within the team to learn about category management in a fun and pragmatic manner without the need to attend intensive category management trainings. You can apply some of the tools individually, but most are useful when confronted with a growth challenge as a team. More and more shopping journeys integrate physical and online touchpoints. The tools can be applied holistically across online and brick-and-mortar stores and they have been tried and tested in different situations and environments. The benefits of this book are that it:

- Contains the main ingredients of the category management concept and practice without the need to attend courses or read more data-intensive books.
- Offers practical suggestions for 1) Analytical review 2) Creative solutions building 3) Energisers for improved collaboration between retailer and suppliers.
- Taps into the need of millennials and other practitioners for transferring knowledge in a highly graphical manner and through appealing and original design.
- Puts the shopper interest first so that retailers and suppliers can work together on category level.
- Represents the latest way of doing things in the field of category management.
- Offers simple frameworks and makes pragmatic suggestions on how to make things work based on my hands-on experience.

How to use the 42 tools of the Retail Innovation Toolkit

Pick up the relevant tool when confronted with a retail growth challenge. These tools offer concrete directions for solutions rather than leaving you with more questions. The idea is to identify ways to grow the category in a quick and enjoyable manner. The tools are designed to support your creative process, to help you to think things through and to collaborate with others while doing so. This is the way the book is structured:

- The toolkit has been divided into seven groups, each with six tools. The tools are numbered and follow a logical order. For example, first you need to define the category strategy before you build the category assortments. That said, you may pick up a specific tool when the need arises.
- Each tool is divided into five sections and is accompanied by a key visual. A tool starts with the description of a context or challenge occurring commonly in the field of category management, which makes it easy to relate to your situation. A clear goal is then stated. Preparations are indicated in relation to any tools, data and/or team setting that you need to have ready in advance. Then, the activity is explained in a succinct, step-by-step manner followed by a description of the desired outcome.
- Each tool tells you how much time you require in the action phase. The estimated duration depends on your experience in the category management field and the composition of your team. To this end, the expected sophistication and experience are signaled for each tool through a star rating whereby basic category management expertise is assumed in the case of one star (*), and very advanced skills in case of five stars (*****).
- Two or more case studies illustrate the retail context in which the tool is applied and give inspiration on how you could adapt the tool to your situation.
- Some of the tools are more applicable to the retailer side than to the supplier side or vice versa, and therefore the user group indicates whether the tool is typically used by R(etailers) and/or S(uppliers). Still, it is interesting to study the tool if you work 'on the other side'.

User Group:	R & S
Challenge Level:	***
Time in Action Phase:	1.5 h

- As you use the tools more frequently, you can start reiterating the order depending on things that need reviewing, evolving and adapting for the context of your retail operation.

This book is the result of the exploration of several knowledge areas over the past 25 years. It would not have been possible without the help of others who shared their thoughts and ideas on retail innovation. Special thanks are owed to three people who provided me with great feedback on an early draft of this book: Carola Verschoor, Linda van Rijn and Rob Mienis. I hope that the application of the tools accelerates your skills in managing categories, mobilising teams across organisations and creating memorable experiences for shoppers. Enjoy!

Tool Index

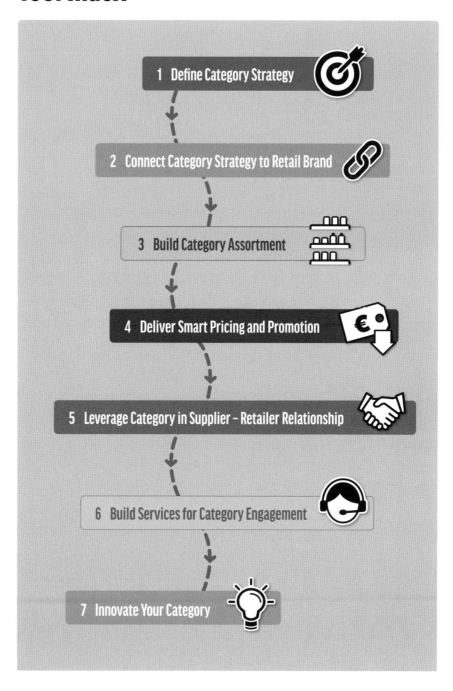

1 Define Category Strategy

2 Connect Category Strategy to Retail Brand

3 Build Category Assortment

4 Deliver Smart Pricing and Promotion

5 Leverage Category in Supplier – Retailer Relationship

6 Build Services for Category Engagement

7 Innovate Your Category

Series 1: Define Category Strategy

Each category has a role to play for the retailer, and for the shopper. Taking into account the characteristics of the category helps define the category strategy that forms the playing field of brands.

In this series of tools, you first define what the category actually is according to the consumer. Next, you define objectives and category strategies that determine how you achieve incremental category growth.

Tools

1. How to define the category
2. How to formulate a category vision
3. How to identify category drivers
4. How to allocate categories to category roles
5. How to assign category strategies
6. How to link category tactics to a category challenge

Series 2: Connect Category Strategy to Retail Brand

Retailers have a choice of where and how to play. How they wish to be perceived is reflected in decisions they make on the category strategy.

Most of the exercises in this series are designed for retailers. They need to understand the benefits of the retail brand in order to make these come alive in day-to-day category management.

Tools

1. How to describe benefits from retail brand
2. How to align my products according to retail brand positioning
3. How to leverage my products to make my brand shine
4. How to find associations with the retail brand
5. How to decide on a national versus a local approach
6. How to get inspiration for category differentiation

Series 3: Build Category Assortment

The shopper's first consideration is what product the retail brand offers. There is an infinite number of alternative approaches to depth, width and quality of assortment that need to be carefully aligned with shopper needs.

Assortment is the second most important driver of store choice after location/accessibility, and therefore product selections are the first step in working out the category management action plan.

Tools

1. How to determine the number of products in the category
2. How to rationalise the assortment
3. How to build a shopper decision tree
4. How to determine missing products
5. How to get ideas for packaging design
6. How to balance competing merchandising objectives

Series 4: Deliver Smart Pricing and Promotion

Increased competition and price transparency require a strong pricing structure that enables flexible decision-making. Providing the shopper value through regular pricing or frequent promotions needs to be evaluated from both brand and profit perspective.

Bounded by the applicable legislation, both supplier and retailer have their own responsibility when it comes to pricing and promotions. Setting the right regular price and choosing the right frequency and depth of promotions makes the category healthy in the long term.

Tools

1. How to select products for price change
2. How to structure my brand portfolio
3. How to enhance category value through packaging size
4. How to find the optimal level of discount
5. How to decide on promotion frequency
6. How to improve promotional decision-making

Series 5: Leverage Category in Supplier – Retailer Relationship

The category can come alive when the relationship between
the supplier and retailer is tight and engaging. Defining the
most suitable role for the category is essential so that the
category story can be told in a congruent and appealing way.
In this series you will learn how to select the right partner and
obtain advice on things you can do to keep the relationship strong.

Tools
1. How to prepare the conversation
2. How to structure the story
3. How to prioritise suppliers
4. How to prioritise retailers
5. How to create differentiated solutions for retailers
6. How to energise the collaboration

Series 6: Build Services for Category Engagement

The shopper perceives services for a physical product as an
integral part of the category solution. Identifying the right
services helps differentiate retail brands and helps create
strategies for more category value.

By researching the shopping journey, you can improve shopper satisfaction.
The exercises help you create new services and store designs.

Tools
1. How to improve the experience of the shopping trip
2. How to identify cues for new services
3. How to discern whether shoppers enjoy time spent
4. How to identify friction and triggers in the shopping tasks
5. How to create ideas for a new store concept
6. How to revisit shopper expectations

Series 7: Innovate Your Category

New stimuli from other markets make shoppers expect every category to evolve. The reference point for new experiences is the best last experience they had in any of the categories they purchase and use. Understanding the emotions and behaviour of shoppers enables brands to proactively foresee future solutions they are likely to prefer. This will keep the category relevant in the future. This last series of tools is oriented towards the future of the category. They help you explore and select new ideas for reinventing your category.

Tools

1. How to phrase shopper arguments
2. How to identify the source of incrementality
3. How to select the best category initiatives
4. How to scope for innovation
5. How to boost the value of a small basket
6. How to bundle new brand ideas into category themes

www.theretailinnovationtoolkit.com

THE RETAIL INNOVATION TOOLKIT

   42 tools

| INSPIRATION | STRATEGY | ACTION | EXPLORE |

FILTER

▼ Define Category Strategy
  1 How to define the category
  2 How to formulate a category vision
  3 How to identify category drivers
  4 How to allocate categories to category roles
  5 How to assign category strategies
  6 How to link category tactics to a category challenge

▶ Connect Category Strategy to Retail Brand

▶ Build Category Assortment

▶ Deliver Smart Pricing and Promotion

▶ Leverage Category in Supplier – Retailer Relationship

▶ Build Services for Category Engagement

▶ Innovate Your Category

1 Define Category Strategy

2 Connect Category Strategy to Retail Brand

3 Build Category Assortment

4 Deliver Smart Pricing and Promotion

5 Leverage Category in Supplier – Retailer Relationship

6 Build Services for Category Engagement

7 Innovate Your Category

THE RETAIL INNOVATION TOOLKIT

OFFLINE

Store

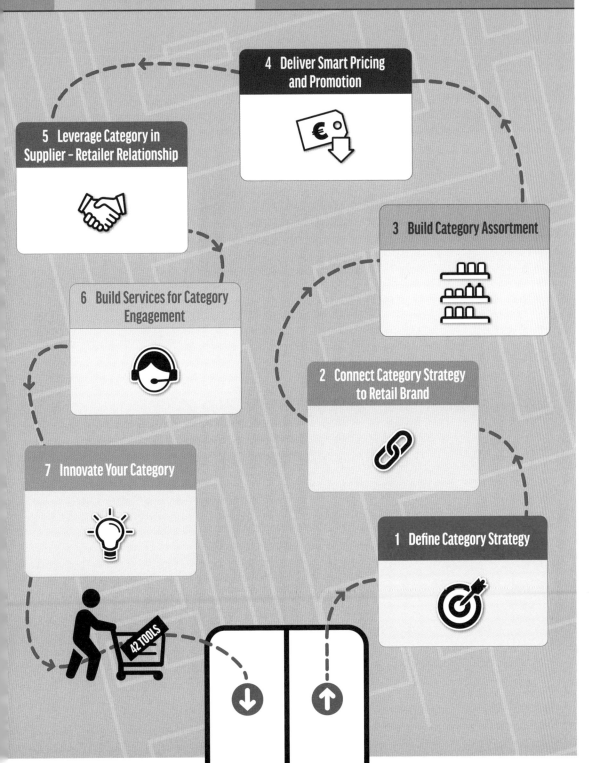

4 Deliver Smart Pricing and Promotion

5 Leverage Category in Supplier – Retailer Relationship

3 Build Category Assortment

6 Build Services for Category Engagement

2 Connect Category Strategy to Retail Brand

7 Innovate Your Category

1 Define Category Strategy

42 TOOLS

1 Define Category Strategy

TOOLS

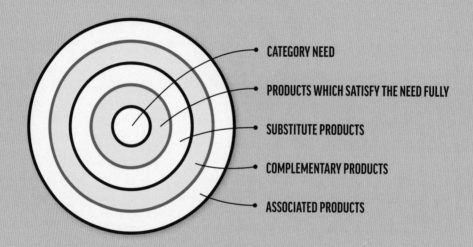

CATEGORY NEED

PRODUCTS WHICH SATISFY THE NEED FULLY

SUBSTITUTE PRODUCTS

COMPLEMENTARY PRODUCTS

ASSOCIATED PRODUCTS

TOOL

How to define the category

User Group:	R & S
Challenge Level:	★★★
Time in Action Phase:	1.5 h

Situation

You wonder where the shopper expects to find the product, as it might fit several categories. To determine where that might be, a thorough understanding of shopper behaviour and motivations is key. As a retailer it is also advisable to deep-dive into shopper perspectives when you (re)define store formats and products. It ensures you (re)assign products to categories in line with the shopping need-states so that expectations are met.

Goal

Define category according to consumer logic.

Preparation

- Start by defining the category need from the perspective of the consumer, based on your research. Write it down on a card, in simple language.
- Use different colours for five A3 cards stating: Category need, Full match, Substitute, Complement, Associated.
- Think of as many product segments as you can that could potentially be part of the category and write these names on the A3 cards.

Action

- Place the category need in the middle of the table or floor. Then, place the five coloured cards around it. Work concentrically from the inside out as shown in the diagram.
- Assign each card with a product name to a circle depending on how it fulfils the need from a consumption perspective.
- When completing the category definition exercise, it is helpful to think of the following oral care example. First you define the category need (clean mouth); next you brainstorm 1) products that satisfy this need (e.g. toothpaste); 2) substitute products (e.g. chewing gum); 3) complementary products (e.g. travel kit); and 4) associated products (e.g. lip balsam).

Outcome

Only products that fully satisfy the need together form the category (inner circle). The others need to be assigned to other categories.

Case in point #1: Products that fit multiple categories

Some products can be assigned to several categories, as in the case of dried apricots: when packaged in a small bag, they are an ideal on-the-go bite; in mixed boxes, they are part of evening nibbles; and when sold loose, they are ingredients for salads. In online retail this is quite easy to organise, simply by assigning them to all categories that apply. But in physical stores, it means double or even multiple placement. This can increase (impulse) sales as retailers give a visible signal to the shoppers through placement in the context of possible use. In the case of apricots, this is by presenting them at checkout, next to nuts and snacks and in the fresh produce section.

Case in point #2: Defining a category for a novel product

The question of category definition also arises when shoppers need to learn where to shop for new products like bags for cold tea or meatless hamburgers.

Case in point #3: Category definition in the context of store format

Category definition also plays a role in defining a store format and assortment selection. For example, a new convenience store that serves only immediate consumption needs will have a soft drinks category that no longer includes family packs of large bottles.

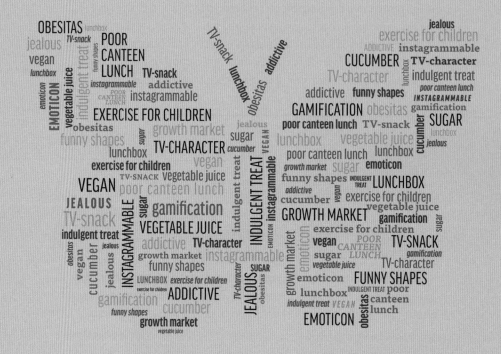

'Three years from now,
one out of three children
will carry a vegetable
snack in their lunch box'

TOOL

2

How to formulate a category vision

User Group:	R & S
Challenge Level:	***
Time in Action Phase:	2.5 h

Situation

You have gone through an elaborate process of researching trends and shopping behaviour. You sprinkled the outcomes with creative energy. You have a fairly good idea where the category is heading but your challenge is to articulate it better.

Goal

Use easy to understand words to describe the future state of the category.

Preparation

- Prepare a summary of category trends, market developments, consumer behaviour and shopper challenges.
- Have space for break-outs in pairs, paper and pens ready.

Action

- Present category trends to team in 1.5 hours max.
- In order to find simple words, role-play in pairs whereby one plays a child asking open-ended questions about the category. Each time the 'child' asks 'why', you dig deeper into what is really important. Conduct different rounds of role-plays.
- Gather as a group and download key words from the role-play into a list. Generate a word cloud using any of the available online tools such as Wordle, WordItOut or similar applications.
- Select the most salient words to create one or two sentences that describe what the category will look like three years from now.
- Describe your category in a short but inspirational statement that represents the essence of where you see the category heading. The best category vision statement can be delivered as an elevator pitch: the objective is to give wings to the message that reaches many people.

Outcome

Inspiring, co-created statement of the category vision.

Case in point #1: Explain the vision in simple language

Microsoft's Bill Gates envisioned 'A computer on every desk and in every home'. We now carry around computers in the form of smartphones in our hands, but in the eighties this was a revolutionary idea.

Case in point #2: Make it purpose-driven

The trend for zero waste is here to stay. Developing a vision for the fruit and vegetable category and making it purpose-driven increases shopper engagement. Lidl supermarkets have introduced reusable nets for the purchase of fruit in-store. By using the nets, shoppers confirm their green credentials as well as the category captainship in fruit and vegetables of this supermarket.

Case in point #3: Assert your thought leadership to create a category of your own

Shoppers are attracted to leading brands because of their innovative way of creatively bringing category visions to life. Such is the case with Uniqlo: a retailer that has created a category unto their own. Their name stands for 'unique clothing' and plays into the trend for affordable clothing. Uniqlo's slogan is 'made for all', and it offers rainbow-coloured fashion for men, women and children. It has become the top fashion retailer in Asia, through a focused vision of simple, affordable, single-coloured fashion items.

CATEGORY ANALYSIS AND EXPERTISE

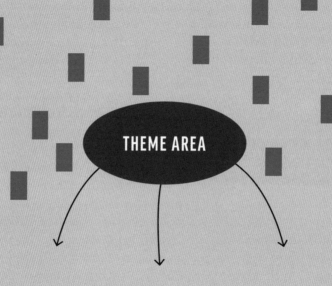

THEME AREA

PATTERNS

CATEGORY DRIVER

TOOL

3

How to identify category drivers

User Group:	R & S
Challenge Level:	****
Time in Action Phase:	1 d

Situation

You are looking for broadly defined category drivers that give inspiration while also activating and giving direction to your category vision. While the category vision sets the direction, the drivers are the carriers that tell how you reach your destination. Sometimes it is easy to see how to make the category more attractive: common drivers are 'better product availability' and 'reduction of choice stress'. In addition to these more obvious candidates for category drivers, it is more inspirational when you identify drivers that are new, more specific to your category, are likely to last for a number of years and have deep impact. In this exercise, you first take a step back by mining so-called theme areas from your data pack. These theme areas could still be worded loosely, but you feel there is something interesting and valuable in them. During the exercise, you may split these theme areas or combine them into something bigger.

Goal

Identify innovative category strategies based on in-depth analysis, your expertise and store safari.

Preparation

- Identify a max of twelve theme areas from your category analysis, for example 'choice stress' or 'young people going to school'.
- Prepare the inspiration room and stick sheets of paper on the wall with category statistics, trends, consumption context images, etc.
- Invite a multifunctional team of six to ten people.

Action

- Work in pairs to formulate the challenge of why the consumer wants to solve the given theme area.
- Organise a store safari around each of the theme areas. Include both online and physical stores.
- Return to the inspiration room. Add sticky notes with the observations of your safari to each theme area on your wall. Also add any new themes if you found new ones.
- Take a step back and look for patterns. Collect sticky notes from any theme area. Alone or combined they become a category driver.

Outcome

A set of five to six category drivers that direct how you achieve the category vision.

Case in point #1: Taste themes and drivers

Within the beer category, lager is routine and price based. Around the edges of the category lies opportunity. The themes and drivers that create preference may include non-standard characteristics like low-alcohol (driver), fruity flavour (driver) as a result of increased consumer health consciousness (theme). An extra step is sustainability (theme) as the example of Lowlander beer shows. This range of beers brewed with botanicals has recently added a non-alcoholic white beer variant. Its citrus flavour is imparted by reclaimed citrus peel from restaurants.

Case in point #2: Consistent product use

Organic cosmetics and hair dyes are on the rise. Many salons that offer vegan and organic products also make sure that attention is given to products for in-home use. In other words, they manage the product lines consistently with the service they offer. Customers don't want to undo at home what they paid a premium for at the salon. So if you have had a plant-based hair dye, the use of organic shampoo and conditioner (category) guarantees that you are consistent in your choice: using plant-based products (theme); for more natural-looking hair (driver) and a healthier scalp (driver).

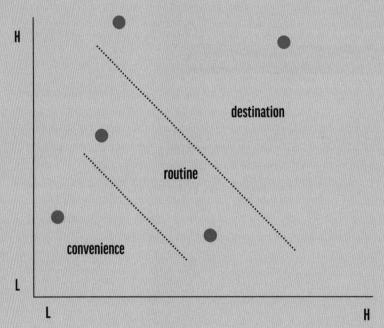

IMPORTANCE TO SHOPPER

H

destination

routine

convenience

L

L   H

IMPORTANCE TO RETAILER

TOOL

4

How to allocate categories to category roles

User Group:	R
Challenge Level:	**
Time in Action Phase:	4 h

Situation

You want to decide on resources and investments depending on the role of the category. Deciding in a less subjective manner on the type of role creates more commitment and makes the effect more permanent. The challenge is how to give the right role to each category, while maintaining a manageable logic. Retailers tend to go through this exercise once in a profound manner and take a soundcheck every year.

Goal

Decide on the role of the category as objectively as possible by collecting facts and views from a broad and diverse number of key stakeholders.

Preparation

- Draw two axes on a sheet of paper or on your digital device. One for the importance of a category for the retailer (horizontal axis) and one for the importance that shoppers attach to it.
- After reviewing the information you collected from stakeholders, select approximately four criteria that constitute shopper importance e.g. category spend by retail target group.
- Select approximately four criteria that constitute retailer importance e.g. category margin.
- Rate each category on a scale of one to ten and calculate average score per category for each of the two axes.
- Plot categories (see example).

Action

- Draw two lines on your chart, as illustrated in the example, creating three groups from the dots you have plotted. The result should be that some 70% of categories are classified in the middle as the routine categories. On the bottom left of the chart, typically about 15% can be classified as convenience, and on the top right, you find destination categories.
- With your team, make any judgement calls you need for the classification of categories to make sense in the logic described.

Outcome

Each category has been assigned a role.

Case in point #1: Regular review of category roles based on data

The role of categories changes continuously; for example, whenever retailers desire a new brand image, when newly launched products change the nature of categories, or when shopping needs evolve. Thus every so often retailers should review the category role model by measuring the importance of the category from both a shopper and a retailer perspective.

When introducing a new supermarket concept, Sainsbury's aimed to increase relevance. First of all, they relocated the bakery category from the back to the front of the store, in order to emphasise their reputation for freshness. Additionally, Sainsbury's tapped into the change in shopper behaviour towards more frequent visits by placing an on-the-go food section in the impulse area of their store thus making it easier for shoppers to find what they sought.

Case in point #2: Change in shopper mission redefines category role

Young urbanites look for ways to design their homes based on high versatility. With the rise in work-from-home, the need to be versatile is even greater, leading to the shoppers' need to find DIY solutions to redesign their home space. Lowe's has traditionally offered products for designing home spaces, but the relevance of home offices allowed them to define a new category role. This was initially tested online, as a soft launch, and as a result of the success in adoption by shoppers, later also rolled out in-store.

(SUB) CATEGORY OBJECTIVE	Market Share	Profit	Return on Assets	Shopper Satisfaction
STRATEGY	**Defend Turf**	**Improve Profit**	**Generate Cash**	**Create Excitement**
	Competitors target these with promotions Frequently purchased Highly price sensitive	Products themselves or others in basket have above average margin High loyalty Low price sensitivity	Products are highly rotating Excellent payment terms Low inventory Efficient supply chain	Category is changing fast Seasons are important Shoppers seek novelty Products with emotional involvement
	Build Traffic	**Build Transaction**		**Enhance Image**
	Products have high household penetration and high market share Could be conserved Price or promotion sensitive	Appeal to larger households Subject to impulse from display Tap into variety seeking Shopper open to volume plus		Products reinforce retail brand: Service, price, quality Loyal shoppers are deeply involved

Overview based on ECR report 'Category Management Best Practices Report', 1997

TOOL

5

How to assign category strategies

User Group:	R & S
Challenge Level:	***
Time in Action Phase:	1 d

Situation

You want to define the role of the subcategories to make sure your category strategy leads to maximum results. A well balanced mix of subcategory strategies will contribute to achieving the category objectives. One of the reasons for this is that your category is composed of different product segments (subcategories), each with their own characteristics.

Goal

Find out if there are subcategories within the category that require a distinct strategy.

Preparation

- Split the category into subcategories.
- Analyse per subcategory: The challenges in terms of market share, profit margin, product segment growth, household penetration, competitive activity, percentage of sales derived from promotion and innovation rate.

Action

- Based on your analysis, assign a category objective to each subcategory.
- Select one or more category strategies for each subcategory.
- Work out detailed action plans by connecting category strategy to plans that the brand marketing team on the supplier side developed.

Outcome

Assignment of objective, strategy and tactics on (sub)category level.

Case in point #1: Analyse whether multiple strategies are relevant

The lighting category in DIY stores like Mr. Bricolage in France are composed of subcategories that align with different shopping behaviours. The market position of the retailer might be different per segment and therefore the same strategy may not work in the same way for all product segments in the category. For example, shoppers buy table lamps on impulse because they are easy to install with a plug and the lampshades follow fashion trends. For this segment a DIY retailer may select an 'excitement creation' strategy. Light bulbs might be 'traffic builders' as they are purchased relatively often and are either purchased as a replacement or for hoarding. Built-in spot lights are purchased as part of a major renovation of the house, and because professional builders are less concerned with the price as they buy on behalf of the consumer, the DIY retailer may select a 'profit strategy' in this case.

Case in point #2: Play into multiple desired outcomes

Shoppers don't always buy products; rather they buy the experiences they want to create with those products. This means that a category is not a one-size-fits-all. A clear example of this is in the body-care category. Large bottles of family-sized soap might fit the 'build transaction' subcategory strategy whereas specific variants such as dry skin or extra hygiene might correspond to 'build profit'. There may also be limited editions that could fit into 'excitement creation'.

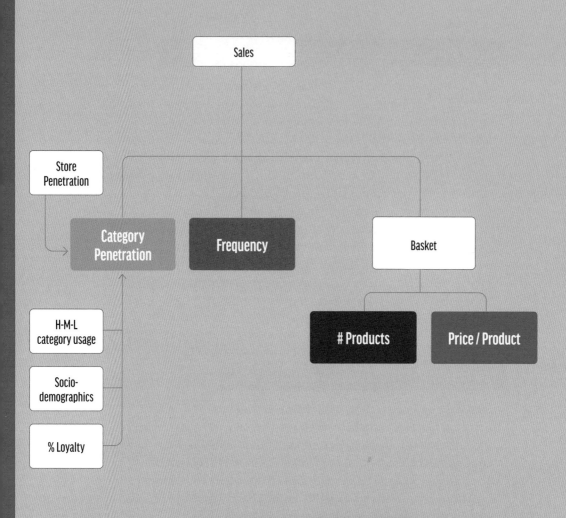

Sales

Store Penetration

Category Penetration

Frequency

Basket

H-M-L category usage

Socio-demographics

% Loyalty

 # Products

Price / Product

1. Identify missing product need
2. Offer all relevant price ranges
3. To which competitor do shoppers go?
4. Repeat last year's deep discount promo

1. Advertise small pack product
2. Work out subscription model if shoppers can predict usage
3. Connect category to other, high- frequency category
4. Set up loyalty promotion program

1. Create new flavours & pack sizes
2. Give discount if shopper buys more
3. Permanent promo deal making people buy one more than previously
4. Raise number of secondary locations

1. Offer variety or special occasion pack
2. Introduce premium range as new price reference
3. Reallocate category space to premium range
4. Promote only premium ranges

TOOL

6

How to link category tactics to a category challenge

User Group:	R & S
Challenge Level:	**
Time in Action Phase:	3 h

Situation

Sales are down. You have ideas about potential causes and you want to make sure you link these to the right category tactics. Your challenge is to win shoppers with a relevant category tactic.

Goal

Generate alternatives to address the sales levels by connecting the category issue with the right marketing tactic.

Preparation

- Analyse the category sales decrease with help of consumer household panel data: number of shoppers, frequency of purchase, number of products in basket, average price.
- Deep dive into actions by specific shopper segments and time periods.
- Split into four teams of two to four people.

Action

- Each team receives a challenge: penetration, frequency, volume or price per product.
- Write down as many ideas to address the challenge – roughly divided into four tactics: product, pricing, place, promotion (see examples of tactics).

Outcome

Menu card of alternative marketing tactics per category issue.

Case in point #1: Addressing sales decline with the help of promotions

When you address a challenge in your category such as decline in revenue, you find the driving force by dividing the sales into four elements: category penetration, frequency, number of products and price. For example, imagine the sales of the fish category declined by 10% compared to the previous year. First, you want to find out if it is a category challenge or a store issue by comparing the overall store performance. If the category decline is caused by a loss of shoppers, you need to find out who they are. A deep discount may trigger them to return to the fish category. However, if on the other hand purchase frequency is the cause, a different promotion mechanism is required such as a loyalty programme. Finally, if the basket size is the cause of the sales decline, you may think of 'buy 2 – get 1 free' offers.

Case in point #2: Use web analytics to pivot your tactics

The rise of online retail allows for detailed analytics and specific actions through SEO (search engine optimisation) and SEA (search engine advertisement). For any retailer, location has always been key, but with online this has become critical. Findability is an important category tactic, referred to as 'local search'. It matters especially in out-of-home outlets, because if they can't find you, they can't buy from you. Take for example Starbucks. If you use a search engine to find a Starbucks store near you, you always find one. Here's why: they have consistent listings ('Starbucks' not 'Starbucks, Inc.' or 'Starbucks Coffee, Inc.'), they use Google My Business pages, and they keep information up to date. Put the other way round, if sales are down for your local café, it is worth exploring whether 'local search' is doing its job in making the store findable.

2 Connect Category Strategy to Retail Brand

TOOLS

1. How to describe benefits from the retail brand
2. How to align my products according to retail brand positioning
3. How to leverage my products to make my brand shine
4. How to find associations with the retail brand
5. How to decide on a national versus a local approach
6. How to get inspiration for category differentiation

TRENDS

OTHER RETAIL
SECTORS

PERCEIVED
PERSONALITY

BENEFITS

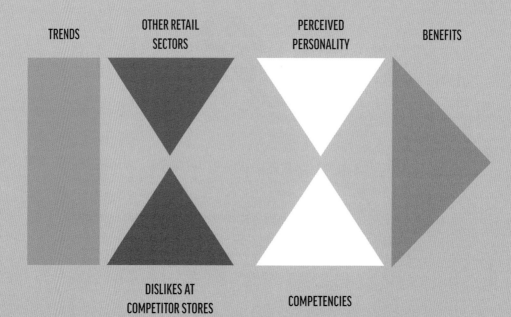

DISLIKES AT
COMPETITOR STORES

COMPETENCIES

TOOL

1

How to describe benefits from the retail brand

User Group:	R
Challenge Level:	****
Time in Action Phase:	4 h

Situation

You want your brand to stand out from the competition and you want to drive shopper preference. A retail brand may want to benchmark itself against others, but this takes you only as far as others have already come. This is not sufficiently differentiating to win preference; scoring yourself on the price is only one way of measuring the brand.

Goal

Define the benefits that shoppers obtain from shopping at your retail brand.

Preparation

Prepare five sources of information to guide your selection of the benefits of the retail brand. Here are some ideas:

1. Read reports on the future well-being of consumers. To ensure you select benefits tapping into trends.
2. Interview shoppers at competitor stores and ask them what they dislike about that store, to find ways to differentiate. Also visit online stores and go through the shopper experience of your competitors to gain insights.
3. Do desk research online to find three successful business models from other retail sectors.
4. Interview your own shoppers to find out how your brand is perceived. Look for analogies that stretch your understanding, for example by asking your shoppers to compare your brand with car brands.
5. Obtain evidence for what makes the retail brand different by asking your staff.

Action

- Based on your preparation, describe three to five functional benefits (e.g. fast delivery) that you wish to deliver to your shoppers.
- Translate these into emotional benefits (e.g. assurance of food when I need it) and connect these with two to ten objectively described competencies (e.g. cooking station at a max of five minutes from each customer).

Outcome

A list of clearly articulated benefits of shopping at your retail brand in shopper language.

Case in point #1: Differentiation is the result of clear choices

Superdrug, a health and beauty retailer in the UK, presents its brand benefits clearly: as a modern brand that stays on top of trends and an affordable store that primarily targets women.

Trends within beauty are an ongoing source of inspiration for shoppers, which Superdrug features on its website as 'trending' to create attention and reassert its image as a beauty retailer. More specifically, playing into the trend towards vegan and animal-free products, Superdrug has introduced a special vegan private label range, B.Cosmetics, and dedicated pop-up stores.

Nonetheless, Superdrug is known for its affordable pricing, so to counter promotional pressure from supermarkets, they must also ensure attractive price-offs are continuously visible to their audience.

Branding is also a matter of choice. In the case of Superdrug, this involves targeting primarily women in their communication. Also, in supporting activities, such as International Women's Day, the brand has a female personality.

Case in point #2: Claim the category benefit at brand level

UK's health and beauty retailer Boots started as a herbalist store in the English town of Nottingham in the mid 1800s. Initially, their own research and the production of painkillers and other drugs gave it a strong medical heritage. Though fighting illness is still an important brand element that is supported through wide on-site availability of pharmacists, the brand now wishes to offer general well-being in response to a more holistic understanding of health by consumers and increasing competition from discount stores. Boots launched one of the first loyalty card programmes, and is known for its generous reward scheme.

FICTIVE EXAMPLE FOR RETAIL BRAND OF BEAUTY PRODUCTS

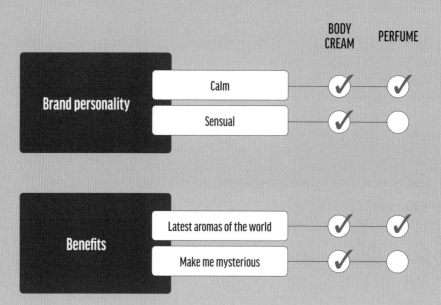

TOOL

2

How to align my products according to retail brand positioning

User Group:	R
Challenge Level:	****
Time in Action Phase:	4 h

Situation

You need to decide on or review the selection of product types and the combination of products that will help build the shopper perception of your retail brand. Within a retail brand, different product categories may be on offer. Thus, the impact of the subcategories on the overall retail brand needs to be deliberately planned.

Goal

Apply a set of brand criteria to ensure you operate in the right subcategories.

Preparation

- Make a list of the benefits and personality of the retail brand.
- Define which subcategories could potentially fit the retail brand, for example by seeking inspiration from the category product hierarchy from (online) retail specialist stores or the products involved in the usage situation.

Action

- Agree on the minimum number of times a subcategory is required to meet the brand statements (✓).
- Select subcategories that fit the brand.
- Within the subcategory, select individual products and brands.

Outcome

Selection of subcategories in which the retail brand should or shouldn't operate.

Case in point #1: Select assortment consistent with brand values and target group

When US pharmacy retailer CVS adopted a new strategy to attract more health-conscious shoppers, it did not just add 'Health' to its corporate name, but also communicated its new purpose through assortment and merchandising. The first step was to ban all tobacco from their stores. CVS Health also moved confectionery and salty snacks from impulse locations at the front of the store to the less attractive centre of the store. The open space was filled with healthier snacks. In the non-food section, it removed personal care products with excessive chemicals.

Case in point #2: Ban products that are not in line with sustainable goals

In 2018 Tesco gave its suppliers a list of requirements to meet if they wished to remain listed in their supermarket. One of the key issues for the supermarket chain is the excessive packaging in consumer products. After researching several categories to assess the amount of plastic packaging and realising that there was much to be improved, Tesco pledged in 2019 to dial up its battle against single-use plastic by banning brands using excessive packaging, particularly non-recyclable plastics. While sustainability is not the core of the Tesco brand, making it a mandatory criterion defines the scope of the category strategy. And in their own words, every little helps. When it comes to the environment too.

POPULAR IN
SOCIAL MEDIA

TELLS THE STORY
IN ONE IMAGE
OR A FEW WORDS

HIGH REACH,
HIGH SHOPPER
PENETRATION

WHAT IS YOUR
RETAIL BRAND ABOUT?

TOOL

3

How to leverage my products to make my brand shine

User Group:	R
Challenge Level:	***
Time in Action Phase:	4 h

Situation

At times it seems each retailer offers the same assortment. And there is simply no way the retailer can offer more products than Amazon or Alibaba. Therefore, your challenge is to look for ways to make current products shine more.

Goal

Identify products in your portfolio that come with a colourful story and therefore provide differentiation.

Preparation

- Rank the top fifty products by basket penetration. This ensures the selection of products are relevant to a large group of shoppers.
- Scan Instagram or Pinterest to see which of these fifty products get talked about in relation to the retail brand.
- Print on A3 paper: retail brand vision & mission, values & beliefs, personality.
- Collect several types of magazines.

Action

- First select products that receive interest from shoppers on Instagram or Pinterest.
- Print Instagram/Pinterest images or cut them from magazines.
- Continue with those products with interesting product heritage that tell where, how and who produced them.
- Validate which stories resonate best with the retail brand.

Outcome

A selection of products that reaches many shoppers, has high human impact and produces a nice story on the shelf label or online.

Case in point #1: Search the products that tell the story of your store

The Dutch gift store WAAR positions itself around beautiful presents with a story. The products range from plants, food, home decoration, beauty products and much more but they share principles of sustainability and fair trade. All the products have a label. Some are highlighted in the store by an additional text card. They tell the story about the plant that filters the air and makes you more creative. Or they point to cooking utensils made from acacia wood sourced from communities in the Philippines that receive a fair payment for their work.

Case in point #2: Great inspiration from fans on social media

Fans of the Dutch home decoration retailer Xenos have made a select number of furniture products, such as the baker's cupboard and the hanging chair, icons of the retail brand by sharing pictures on Pinterest and other social media. In a social media driven and spontaneous manner, they help each other to get to know the brand, and as a result of their enthusiasm, help shape the brand.

SURVEY QUESTIONS FOR SHOPPERS

1. Mention three organisations that come to mind when you think of [category name / retail sector].

2. Do you know [retail brand name]?

3. Mention three things that come to mind when you think of [retail brand name]?

4. Circle four words that you think best fit [retail brand name]? *{show paper with max thirty words}*

5. To which degree do you think the following personality traits fit [retail brand name]? *{Allow interviewees to add words they think are missing}*

TOOL

4

How to find associations with the retail brand

User Group:	R
Challenge Level:	**
Time in Action Phase:	2 d

Situation

You want to build maximum relevance into your proposition. Prices have never been as transparent and availability of products has never been as high. By knowing what makes your retail brand distinct, you can tailor the product offering, appeal to a special audience, drive communication and define any other tactics.

Goal

Identify whether shoppers perceive the brand as you intend.

Preparation

- Collect four to six actions/nouns that are crucial for what you think the brand should reflect (e.g. friendly staff). On a piece of paper, write down a maximum of thirty words that are relevant to your retail sector.
- Collect four to six personality traits of the brand (e.g. humorous).
- Draft a short five minute survey (see example).
- Work with teams of ten.
- Select 'neutral' locations for interviews such as shopping malls and railway stations (also if you work for a pure online player). Each interviewer should intercept twenty shoppers for short interviews.

Action

- Conduct (10 x 20 =) 200 interviews.
- Aggregate and visualise the data.
- Gather as a team and discuss what confirms your beliefs and what surprises you. Where do you see gaps? Explore potential explanations. Analyse how this differs from what you intend and how you might close the perception gap.

Outcome

Description of how shoppers perceive the retail brand.

Case in point #1: Intercept your shoppers

Conducting your own market research – gathering information first hand – always provides insights, especially for small brick-and-mortar retailers. Or in the case of pure digital retailers, it may provide a means to get live contact with your shoppers. In addition, as brands win and lose customers to competition on a continuous basis it is also important to hear from people that have stopped visiting you, or are about to leave you, or have never considered you as an alternative to their current set of brands. In the lean start-up methodology, this is referred to as 'getting out of the building'. Two best practices in the high street include: interviewing passers-by and briefly inquiring why they didn't shop at your store and visiting the competitor's store and asking shoppers what led them to choose that specific store at the moment of the intercept.

Case in point #2: Defining your brand in highly competitive markets

When people shop for music in France, they may mention online retailer Amazon, Carrefour Hypermarket or Spotify. Perhaps they did not think of entertainment retailer Fnac immediately, though this retailer has a good presence both online and offline. Therefore, you first ask for associations that come to mind right away, such as friendly staff and cultural inhouse events. Next you want to provoke responses on brand associations by asking if buyers and non-buyers think Fnac has fast online delivery and a flexible return policy. Some of these services have become industry standards so therefore it is helpful to find out how the brand personality (agile? fair? humorous?) of the Fnac brand compares to others.

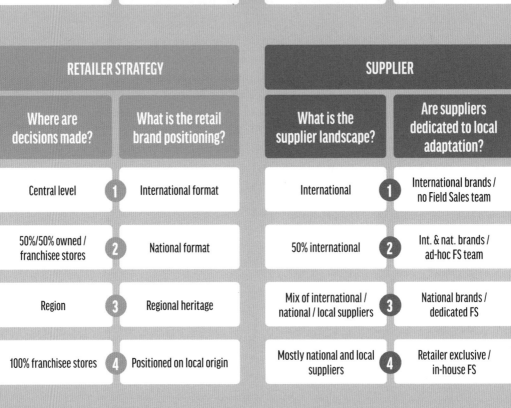

CATEGORY

Where does production occur?		On which level is demand variation observed?
National	**1**	Category / National
Regional	**2**	Category / Region
Local preparation	**3**	Segment / Store
Local innovation	**4**	Product / Store

STORE

What is the store function & size variety?		What does promotion look like?
1 format 1-2 sizes	**1**	National
2 formats 2-3 sizes	**2**	Cluster
3 formats 6-8 sizes	**3**	Store
>3 formats >8 sizes	**4**	Personal offer

RETAILER STRATEGY

Where are decisions made?		What is the retail brand positioning?
Central level	**1**	International format
50%/50% owned / franchisee stores	**2**	National format
Region	**3**	Regional heritage
100% franchisee stores	**4**	Positioned on local origin

SUPPLIER

What is the supplier landscape?		Are suppliers dedicated to local adaptation?
International	**1**	International brands / no Field Sales team
50% international	**2**	Int. & nat. brands / ad-hoc FS team
Mix of international / national / local suppliers	**3**	National brands / dedicated FS
Mostly national and local suppliers	**4**	Retailer exclusive / in-house FS

TOOL
5

How to decide on a national versus a local approach

User Group:	R & S
Challenge Level:	**
Time in Action Phase:	2 h

Situation

For brick-and-mortar retailers and their suppliers, new technologies can help solve the riddle of personalisation versus cost-effectiveness. However, the question of whether sales of local and personalised solutions outweigh the benefits of a more centralised approach needs to be approached systematically. There is no one-size-fits-all conclusion.

Goal

Determine how much fertile breeding ground there is for the category to offer more personal and local solutions.

Preparation

- Define the challenge at hand; for example, deciding on local store assortments.
- Define criteria from four perspectives: Category, Store, Retail Strategy and Supplier.

Action

- Answer the eight questions in the overview. Assign points to each answer.
- In total (8 x 4 =) 32 points can be distributed. When a category receives 26 points, a local approach over a standardised approach is recommended.

Outcome

Assessment of whether it makes sense to create local and personalised category solutions.

Case in point #1: Bake-off makes trade-off

Freshly baked bread and pastries are a premium offering in most supermarkets. Such is the case for SPAR supermarkets as well. The SPAR branded bake-off solution is fully customisable to the needs of each individual store. The local aspect is delivered partly by the freshness and partly by the fact that the local stores select their choice from a broad assortment available to all stores. This delivers a great trade-off between high service and high efficiency.

Case in point #2: Ready-made meals fully adapted to local situation

The ready-made meals category could be delivered in the same way across a given country or be highly differentiated per region or area. The arguments for a local approach versus a national approach are stronger if the ready-made meals category can be described as follows: 1) chefs in individual stores have the freedom to develop their own recipes; 2) demand for types of cuisine is dependent on preferences in the catchment area; 3) the retailer can tailor the most suitable retail format (e.g. dark kitchen, convenience store, take-away) to the local situation; 4) the retailer applies personalised offers; 5) the franchise operated system stimulates local entrepreneurship; 6) the retail brand image is famous for taking into account local preferences; 7) an ecosystem of suppliers around each store favours fast delivery of ingredients; 8) all products and brands are 100% owned by the retailer.

MARKETING TACTIC	Which retail format does the shopper consider a relevant proposition for this category specifically with regard to this attribute?	Will the category offer less value, perform equally, or will the category offer differentiating value?	If you deliver differentiating value, how can the shopper experience this in the category?
PRICE	Name of Retailer = ...	Less / Same / More	Explain = ...
ASSORTMENT			
MERCHANDISING			
STAFF			
MOBILE / WEBSITE			
EXPERIENCE			
ACCESS / LOCATION			
CONVENIENCE			
SUSTAINABILITY			
DESIGN			

TOOL

6

How to get inspiration for category differentiation

User Group:	R
Challenge Level:	**
Time in Action Phase:	2 h

Situation

You want your marketing efforts to have maximum effectiveness. A successful category proposition is both relevant to the shopper and is different from the competition. The same category can be purchased at different formats, so the distinct benefits a retail format offers need to be clear.

Goal

Identify the relevant benchmark per marketing tactic/category level.

Preparation

- Collect inspiring material in the form of retailer magazines, store images and website screenshots.
- Work with the complete category management team.

Action

- Complete the table (see example) in three steps.
- Column 1: Indicate which format is a relevant benchmark. This can be different per marketing tactic.
- Column 2: Decide per marketing tactic whether your aim is for the category to perform worse, equally or better.
- Column 3: If you decide to outperform, use the sources of inspiration to come up with ideas for what your (new) marketing tactic looks like.

Outcome

Table with levels of benchmark and desired marketing tactics for the selected category.

Case in point #1: Provide a reference to help frame the category

A digital player such as Amazon or a department store such as Macy's are examples of stores that sell many different categories under one (digital) roof. When the number of categories increases, it becomes increasingly difficult for them to demonstrate to shoppers that they have expertise in each of these. Therefore, Amazon could list the most relevant and inspiring competitor for different aspects of the category. For example, Amazon may include Primark as the benchmark for price and Everlane for sustainability. Amazon may think they perform equally to Zalando when it comes to speed of delivery and customer service. Despite its wide range, it may score itself average on assortment because shoppers do not consider the products fashionable. Therefore, Amazon may seek help from famous haute couture designers to create a brand of products sold exclusively on its platform.

Case in point #2: Seek inspiration from the best in the class

Carrefour Planet was a store concept for hypermarket giant Carrefour. In these stores, the aim was to create an ambience for each category, based on referential concepts that sought to compete with the strongest retailer in each category. The reference became La Grande Épiceries for fresh Produce, leading to choices in bulk presentation, in-store counters, use of aprons instead of uniforms for personnel, presentation with fresh plants in-store and similar cues. Fast fashion stores served as the reference for textiles, changing the way collections were presented, although through the use of referencing it also became clear that they could not truly compete with specialist brands so space for textiles was reduced by 12%.

3 Build Category Assortment

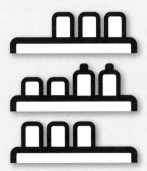

Tools

1. How to determine the number of products in the category

2. How to rationalise the assortment

3. How to build a shopper decision tree

4. How to determine missing products

5. How to get ideas for packaging design

6. How to balance competing merchandising objectives

Show outcomes of your research:

low   high

1. SHOPPER PERCEPTION

2. RETAIL POSITIONING   If shopper perception of variety is not aligned with retail brand (   )
                        positioning, you may want to increase the actual number of products

3. ACTUAL NUMBER

● Retail brand
● Competitor brands

DISCUSS TOGETHER:

1. Can warehouse space be amended? Or are supply chain savings more important to the organisation?

2. Do additional products justify the increase of supply chain costs? Or can you find ways to increase incremental sales?

3. Can products be replenished anytime to free up space for variety? Or are labour costs in-store too high?

4. Is assortment size an important instrument to compete? Or are other marketing instruments more effective?

5. Will increasing the actual number of products result in higher shopper satisfaction? Or can we improve category performance through other assortment tactics?

6. Do the incremental sales from this category outperform sales from other categories? Or do you have a good business case?

TOOL

1

How to determine the number of products in the category

User Group:	R & S
Challenge Level:	***
Time in Action Phase:	4 h

Situation

You want to decide how many products to include in your category. The optimal number of products in the category depends on a large number of variables such as retail brand positioning. And as markets are dynamic, the number varies in time. The challenge is that you need to compete with Amazon but cannot offer an infinite number of products.

Goal

Identify the number of products in the category that is right for your retail brand.

Preparation

- Conduct shopper research and probe for perception of assortment variety versus categories at competitor retail brands.
- Count number of products in key planograms at main competitors.
- Invite experts from Insights, Store Operations, Supply Chain and Commercial teams.

Action

- There is no mathematically correct answer, therefore the team agrees on a weighted scoring of decision factors: 1) warehouse space; 2) store operation costs/space (only for brick-and-mortar); 3) retail brand/benchmarking; 4) shopper satisfaction/availability.
- The advised order is to start with the assortment perceptions of the shopper. Next you check if these perceptions match retail positioning and if shopper perceptions match actual numbers. These facts form the basis of the team discussion on where you want and can implement change.

Outcome

Alignment in the organisation on the number of products in the category.

Case in point #1: Partnering for careful analysis by category

The immediate availability of up to 150.000 items is a key reason for shoppers to visit Walmart stores. However, even Walmart cannot compete with Amazon's endless virtual shelves and convenient shopping from the couch. And Walmart doesn't have the resources to manage all categories in detail as data and analytics are not always readily available. Nonetheless, Walmart must assess which categories drive frequent visits to stores, and importantly, generate sales across categories. To do so, they share the responsibility with suppliers, who need Walmart to reach their customers and thus are relevant partners in the success of the categories. The suppliers have access to the sales data per product, per store and per hour through the Retail Link software. In this way, they can provide Walmart with a careful analysis per category that can inform Walmart's decisions on the number of products and category relevance.

Case in point #2: A flow of ever-changing selections

Another way of thinking about assortment size is to fluctuate the offer while keeping the size of assortment constant. TK Maxx is an excellent case in point. They change their assortment of gift, fashion and personal care almost daily, leaving even store managers to sometimes wonder what the next delivery will bring. And so everyone is prepared for the unexpected. For store managers, this involves thinking in terms of flow rather than static assortment. And for shoppers, the combination of well-known brands, high discounts versus department stores and the continuous inflow of new products provides the sensation of a great treasure hunt. As a result, apart from basic clothing, most items represent current season styles available in varying quantities.

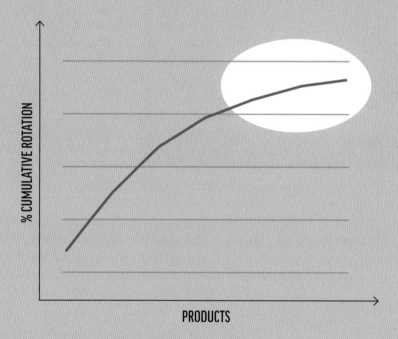

TOOL
2

How to rationalise the assortment

User Group:	R & S
Challenge Level:	*
Time in Action Phase:	2 h (*)

(*) Excl. store pilots

Situation

You need to delist some products from a given category. The category looks cluttered and shoppers complain about having difficulties making a choice from the assortment. It feels as if there is too much duplication but the challenge is how to decide which products can be eliminated from the category.

Goal

Explore whether a reduction in the number of products results in higher shopper satisfaction and sales.

Preparation

- Collect (non-promoted) rotation data per product including number of stores selling and number of weeks the product was offered in-store.
- Rank (non-promoted) rotation per store per week.

Action

- Plot a Pareto curve. For this you sort products starting with best rotating product. Next you calculate cumulative rotation when you add the second-best rotating product, and so on. The cumulative rotation is displayed on the vertical axis.
- Decide whether the products in the tail meet a need-state or shopper group unserved by other products.
- Execute store pilots by reducing the number of products by 15% and 25% and track impact on category basket penetration, sales and profits (this will take an additional two to three months).

Outcome

Decision on which assortment reduction works most optimally for the category.

Case in point #1: Identify the type of needs served by the category

By analysing shopping behaviour with help of loyalty card data, Carrefour in France identified which products served the same shopping need. As a result, Carrefour made significant changes with regard to the number of products, the level of variety and space allocated to the category. For example, Carrefour reduced the number of fruit and vegetable products by 5% overall, but increased the variety by 5% and space by 33%.

Case in point #2: Regular health checks required

Tesco had added so many products that shoppers became stressed from having to make choices in mundane categories. In 2015 the assortment size of 90.000 items had become larger than what shoppers sought, and was certainly larger compared to what competitor supermarkets would offer: Asda and Sainsbury's had 30.000 items available and Aldi some 2.000. For example, Tesco offered 28 alternatives for ketchup while only one was available at Aldi. As a result of this simple reality check, Tesco cut the assortment by 30% to make shopping easier and, at the same time, reduced the costs of warehousing and distribution.

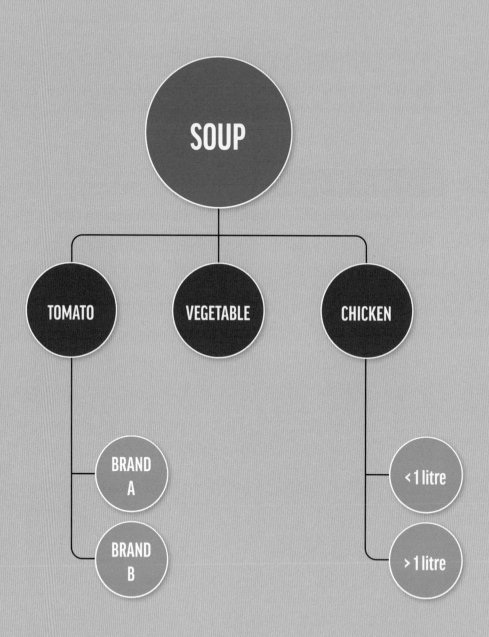

TOOL

3

How to build a shopper decision tree

User Group:	R & S
Challenge Level:	**
Time in Action Phase:	2 d

Situation

Your research shows that shoppers find the presentation of the category too complex. And you want to check for need-states that you forget to serve. In the absence of (loyalty card) data, you wish to create a category structure that is simple to navigate and find products.

Goal

Translate the way shoppers make decisions into the way the category is merchandised.

Preparation

- Select approximately forty participants who buy the category frequently, or in the case of irregularly purchased products, shoppers that are preparing their purchase.
- Ask permission to use a (online) store environment.
- Prepare a list of potential category attributes.

Action

- At the beginning of the shopping trip, ask which attributes they have already decided on before purchase.
- Observe shoppers from the moment they enter the (online) store.
- After purchase, probe for attributes they applied in order to make their decision. Let them rank attributes on your list.
- Ask what would happen if the selected product had been out of stock.
- Aggregate the shopper data to describe the decision order of attributes based on what they indicated.

Outcome

Category structure that describes the hierarchy of product segments in accordance with shopper logic.

Case in point #1: Reflect the shopper decision tree in merchandising

With the help of shopper analysis, the bakery brand Sara Lee found out that organising the aisle first by occasion, such as 'grilling' and 'breakfast', was more effective than organising the aisle by any other aspect. Signage on top of the shelves communicated where each segment could be found. The segments were split following shopper logic, by type of bread, such as hamburger buns, muffins and traditional loaves. As a result, the number of brands per segment was reduced. Insight into which segments were purchased together helped retailers to rearrange the order of segments in the aisle.

Case in point #2: Vary the decision tree by shopper segment

Shoppers of baby milk are emotionally involved in making the best choice for their baby. They perceive strong, well-known brands as great ways to reduce the risk and complexity. Once they have gathered and analysed a lot of information, they usually develop a preference for one brand. Therefore, the shopper decision tree of young parents often starts with the brand followed by criteria such as baby age and flavour. In my own analysis, I found out that parents are prepared to take on more risk after a couple of months: the importance of brand decreases and things like promotions or variety of formats gain relevance.

SALES IN THE MARKET VERSUS % DISTRIBUTION AT RETAILER

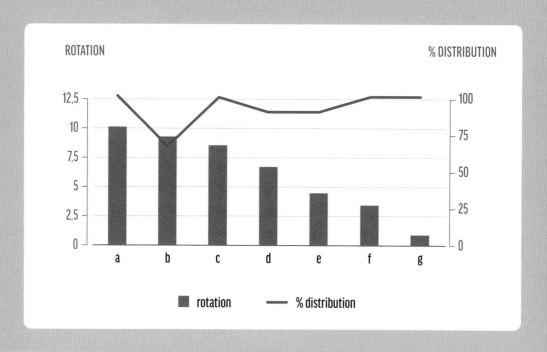

TOOL

4

How to determine missing products

User Group:	**R & S**
Challenge Level:	*
Time in Action Phase:	**4 h**

Situation

You want to find out whether you are carrying successful products with (too) low levels of distribution. If the innovation rate is low or if listing more products is not possible, attention shifts towards optimisation of the current products and their distribution. Whereas you might actually have winners in your assortment but not be giving them all the distribution they deserve. Applicable for brick-and-mortar stores with local assortments and online stores with multiple views across shopper groups.

Goal

Explore whether there are hidden high-performing products.

Preparation

- Gather data on sales (rotation, revenue, volume) per product at the retail brand and aggregated on market level.
- Next, determine the percentage of distribution for the brick-and-mortar retailer: number of stores selling the product divided by total number of stores. Online brands may work with potential number of shoppers across views.

Action

- Plot retail sales and distribution in one graph.
- Identify products that are relatively low in distribution in your retail brand but do well in terms of sales.
- Make an additional check by comparing the sales ranking in the retail brand with sales in the total market.
- Calculate the additional sales/profit resulting from changing the product mix.

Outcome

A recalibrated product offering based on performance within your retail brand and in the market.

Case in point #1: Compare with the competition or think of target group

There are several starting points for exploring which products are missing in your assortment such as shopper complaints at customer service, retail sales databases (e.g. Nielsen), or reviews about the brand and competitors on social media. Another way of looking at this is by analysing preferences of your (potential) customers. For example, when expats from the UK live close to the grocery store make sure you offer Marmite and PG Tips tea. Another example is that Tesco offers some 200 typical Polish food products in the UK.

Case in point #2: Learn what's missing through brand leadership

Many webshops have developed into platforms, leading to a concentration in the online distribution channels. Offering products from third parties also provides the opportunity to track preferences and what is actually bought, showing the platform owner where opportunities lie for increasing their own assortment. It is estimated that more than two billion people worldwide use online stores and the number is expected to continue to grow. And that also makes it interesting to look at what's missing from the lens of the brand, as is the case of Away, a direct to consumer luggage and travel company. They started with the perfect suitcase, then built from there, creating a communication platform on travel stories through podcasts, city guides, travel essays, and photo journals. Through this they redefined their business: it became not only about selling luggage but about offering all manner of articles a traveller needs. Their brand leadership led to a dialogue with their users that allowed them to see what was missing.

TOOL

5

How to get ideas for packaging design

User Group:	R & S
Challenge Level:	***
Time in Action Phase:	8 h

Situation

Your challenge is to design an attractive packaging format as a value alternative to the leading A-brands. Most retailers do not have the resources to develop completely new and one hundred percent original packaging designs for their new products in routine categories.

Goal

Determine packaging characteristics that are important cues in the category.

Preparation

- Ask for help from twenty shoppers, or from friends or family who shop the category regularly.
- Subscribe to software that predicts what people see in the first five seconds of viewing the packaging, such as 3M Visual Attention Software.[2]

Action

- Let people draw packaging of A-brand leaders. With this you obtain cues on important category and attribute characteristics.
- Next you draw a sketch of your packaging.
- To validate your design, use a software tool that applies learnings from academics and other packaging.

Outcome

Rough design for the value alternative of leading A-brands that can be used to brief your graphic department or agency.

---

2 https://www.3m.com/3M/en_US/visual-attention-software-us/

Case in point #1: Measuring impact of packaging in context

Walgreens in the US changed the glass doors of the refrigerators and freezers into screens displaying the product, price and advertising. Sensors detect when shoppers approach the smart glass doors and select a product. In combination with information about weather and time of day, they allow real-time A/B testing of product packaging, but they also enable automated stock control, dynamic pricing and context dependent advertising displayed on the doors.

Case in point #2: Evolving packaging design while keeping brand cues

Since the first Heinz condiments entered the market, the brand has continuously evolved its appearance to ensure saliency. The first condiments were packaged in glass bottles to signal the purity of the ingredients. Nowadays most Heinz ketchup products in supermarkets are packaged in plastic, yet the wide shaped bottle and small product label are still kept to maintain the visual impact of the original see-through tomato bottle. This is further enhanced by the label itself, which is responsive to the modernisation of graphic communication and visual cues, but continues to enhance brand character through the illustration of a growing plant and key references such as 'grown not made' and '57 varieties'.

ALTERNATIVE MERCHANDISING OBJECTIVES

1. Maximise total category profits

2. Maximise total number of products sold

3. Increase cross-selling through complementary products

4. Make product search easy and fast

5. Surprise shoppers with needs/products they had not thought about

6. Offer a core range to satisfy a wide range of needs

7. Reduce operational store costs

8. Reduce warehousing and distribution costs

9. Tailor the assortment to individual and/or local needs

10. Give priority to specific (private label) ranges

11. Avoid out-of-stock whatever it takes

12. Offer alternative product if out-of-stock

13. Enhance the retail brand positioning

14. Offer the widest possible assortment to satisfy the maximum number of shoppers and needs

15. Launch the latest innovations fast

TOOL

6

How to balance competing merchandising objectives

User Group:	R & S
Challenge Level:	**
Time in Action Phase:	4 h

Situation

You wish to make your merchandising objectives unequivocal. Making sure expectations are discussed upfront in the team helps to avoid misunderstandings. Space managers on both retailer and supplier side often struggle to find space for products, because there are too many alternative products available, and because each functional department has different and most likely competing objectives. Your aim is to have a reference to guide decisions for all.

Goal

Establish criteria for merchandising to drive efficient decision-making.

Preparation

Conduct interviews on the importance of assortment and merchandising objectives and let functional teams from finance, sales, brand marketing and trade marketing make rankings. Examples of merchandising objectives are given in the overview.

Action

- Meet as a team and discuss the rankings that the teams prepared for their function.
- Each functional team explains why their objectives are important.
- Agree on one common set of criteria for ranking in your organisation, combined with weights per objective.

Outcome

Weighted mix of criteria for (category) merchandising that forms starting point for project with trade partners.

Case in point #1: Visibility of inventory crucial for category profits

In the eighties, Zara and H&M disrupted the fashion retail market by offering fashionable clothes only four weeks after models showed the latest designs on the catwalks, whereas it took traditional retailers up to five months. Now they are under pressure from ultra-fast fashion players such as Boohoo and ASOS. The latter have similar or even faster times from product design to store merchandising, but on top of that they also produce in very small batches, creating a sense of variety. Flexible supply chains and continuous sales monitoring keep inventories low. If the product is successful, they can increase production fast. In response, Zara and H&M have increased the number of collections to sixteen to twenty per year. Keeping a close eye on inventory across all outlets is crucial for them to avoid expensive markdowns.

Case in point #2: Blended retailing integrates experience and transaction

Space in brick-and-mortar retail is too small to cater to shopper expectations of 100% availability of the widest possible variety of products in all outlets. This often causes out-of-stocks. As a result, the shoppers immediately consult their mobile devices and order elsewhere online. At best, they might switch to similarly priced substitutes in-store, and at worst they simply delay or forget the purchase altogether. This is why blended models have started to appear in a variety of brick-and-mortar outlets: understanding that shoppers want to 'see' the product before they buy, they use their exhibition space smartly for inspiration and then offer touchscreens to buy right then and there, while offering the convenience of having the product shipped to the customer's door. Such is the case of Nike stores who successfully use touchscreens that lead shoppers who are captive in their store environment to their own branded e-commerce platform, multiplying sales both online and in-store.

4 Deliver Smart Pricing and Promotion

TOOLS

1. How to select products for price change

2. How to structure my brand portfolio

3. How to enhance category value through packaging size

4. How to find the optimal level of discount

5. How to decide on promotion frequency

6. How to improve promotional decision-making

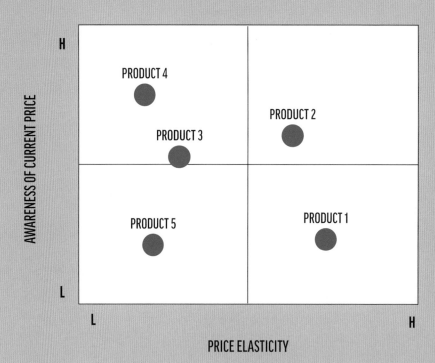

TOOL
1

How to select products for price change

User Group:	R & S
Challenge Level:	**
Time in Action Phase:	2 h

Situation

You want to check whether the price for your products is set at the right level. Pricing is a versatile instrument to create impact fast. Price elasticity (the change of volume after a price change) is important but should not be the only variable in decision-making. The awareness of prices is a key determinant in the shoppers' response. If people are aware, the speed of the reaction will be greater and they will notice the change.

Goal

Determine whether a price change makes sense.

Preparation

- The starting point is research that you conduct on both price elasticity and shopper knowledge of the regular price of the top fifteen products. Some considerations:
  - If prices fluctuated in the past, historic retail scanning data is good input for research.
  - Shopper surveys offer an alternative method when you test new price ranges.

Action

- Plot the products on two axes: awareness of current price and price elasticity.
- Consider future adaptation of price only on products where shoppers are aware of the current price level as they will notice the change and act accordingly, and if there is a significant volume change – either more volume at a lower price or less volume at a higher price. Small changes in volume are too much effort for limited return.

Outcome

Suggestions for optimal price (range) to be used as guidance in brand manual, purchasing and promotional tactics.

Case in point #1: Actual versus perceived price image

The electronics category at MediaMarkt suffered from the increasing offer of the same products in online channels with full transparency of the price to the shopper. MediaMarkt countered the pure digital players with an omnichannel approach including its own webstore. In addition, they went head-on in terms of pricing. They implemented electronic shelf labels in all their stores so that they could respond immediately to competitor price changes. For example, in the Netherlands they scraped the websites of 25 self-chosen competitors to guarantee the best price. Consumer reports showed they got it right many times; however, shopper price image did not concur with the actual prices. Lately, MediaMarkt has removed the price guarantee on the website and aims to reposition itself as a price-orientated service retailer.

Case in point #2: A/B testing to understand the reason behind the price elasticity

Price elasticity is one of the measures that show whether shoppers think products generate value for them. If a price increase elicits a strong drop in demand, it could be that the product is not an essential good and is regarded as a commodity. Some categories tend to be more price sensitive than others; for example, laundry detergents in supermarkets due to the high out-of-pocket expense. Within a category, there could also be large differences. For example, a regular-sized detergent is suitable for promotions and price changes whereas a speciality detergent for stain removal benefits more from everyday low prices. Despite all the data analysis, price elasticities are not stable, exact numbers. For example, elasticity is higher when shoppers have low incomes and when they are half way through their shopping trip. Setting up experiments in different contexts helps to get a number and also to understand why shoppers responded the way they did.

PRICE RANGES →

% OF PRODUCTS (OR SALES) →

TOOL
2

How to structure my brand portfolio

User Group:	R
Challenge Level:	**
Time in Action Phase:	3 h

Situation

You wonder if your retail brand competes effectively with all types of competitors in the market. One of the first factors you want to check is whether you offer products in all relevant price ranges to avoid 'leakage' to competitors. Note: even if the retail brand competes in only one price segment - such as premium or the opposite, as discount brand - understanding of volume implications can be useful.

Goal

Align your product offering with various price segments in the market.

Preparation

- Identify the price at which products in the category are offered in the market. Rule of thumb says this pricing range can be divided into three price segments: good – better – best. However, more or fewer price segments are possible.
- Decide on the exact price levels of these price segments.
- A certain price segment could play a relatively large role in a specific channel/brand format. In those cases you need to check whether your shoppers visit this channel/format often.

Action

- Use the vertical axis for the price levels. Calculate the percentage of products (or percentage sales from those products) that fall into each of the price ranges.
- Discuss whether the structure of your product offer 1) covers the relevant price ranges; 2) resonates with your retail brand; 3) meets category objectives; 4) competes well with other formats and channels.

Outcome

A visual rendering of the shape of your product pyramid per price segment to understand whether you compete with a sufficient number of products in the right price segments.

Case in point #1: Tiered pricing to fight discount

The Tesco own label started as Tesco Value, an inexpensive range of products, just after the recession of the early nineties and as a weapon in the supermarket price war. This has evolved into a tiered own label strategy: budget labels by Tesco prevent the loss of shoppers to Aldi and Lidl, the Tesco brands target leading A-brands, and Tesco Finest, now the UK's largest grocery brand, serves premium desires. Currently, Tesco pays much attention to the budget price range. In 2016 Tesco replaced the Everyday Value range for produce and meat with fictitious names unrelated to Tesco and made associations with British farming villages. Later, the Everyday Value range was phased out in favour of non-Tesco named exclusive discount brands, a strategy that Tesco copied from Aldi and Lidl.

Case in point #2: Premium offer in indulgent biscuit category

How this strategy plays out in practice is illustrated by Tesco's biscuit category. Here Tesco offers some 170 products from 33 brands. From the assortment analysis, we draw the conclusion that Tesco wants to cater to a wide range of needs with a large number of brands, and that shoppers are prepared to pay premium prices. At the moment of analysis, the category could be divided into five price tiers: 8% of the products cost less than £0.50, 18% between £0.50 and £1.00, 19% at £1.00, 35% between £1.00 and £2.00, and 20% above £2.00. This shows a bias towards the premium price tier, which is amplied by the fact that 25% of the brands play in the premium segment and the number of private label products is moderate at 30%. The Tesco Finest range operates only in the most expensive price tier. Finally, Tesco's Ms Molly's range is offered in most tiers apart from the premium tier and the Tesco brand works in all ranges.

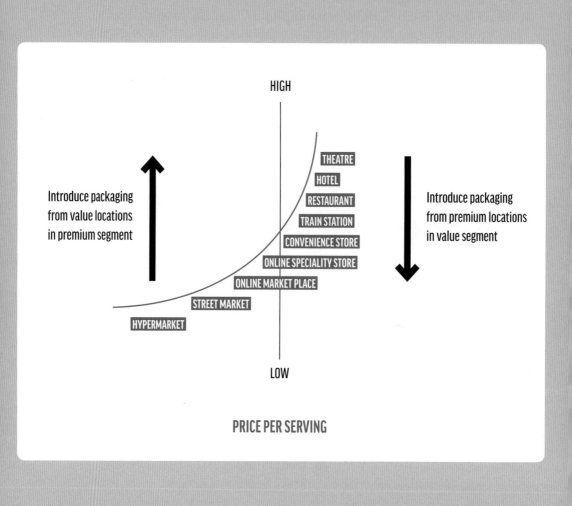

HIGH

Introduce packaging
from value locations
in premium segment

THEATRE
HOTEL
RESTAURANT
TRAIN STATION
CONVENIENCE STORE
ONLINE SPECIALITY STORE
ONLINE MARKET PLACE
STREET MARKET
HYPERMARKET

Introduce packaging
from premium locations
in value segment

LOW

PRICE PER SERVING

TOOL

3

How to enhance category value through packaging size

User Group:	R & S
Challenge Level:	**
Time in Action Phase:	4 h

Situation

You want to keep the category dynamic in a relatively easy manner. Breakthrough innovation is not always the best option because category needs are very functional or perhaps you are encountering organisational barriers. At such times implementing new packaging formats that you may already offer to other customers may be more relevant and effective.

Goal

Maintain category attractiveness for shopper and retailer through packaging innovation (format, size, presentation).

Preparation

- Measure the price of the same product across different locations of purchase types. The number of products you include is optional, but the top ten products of the category are suggested.
- Take photos at the retail location for later, as further inspiration.
- Set up a table in Excel that includes the following information per product: price per serving, grams/litres per serving, price per gram/litre, type of packaging.

Action

- Conclude from your Excel table where large price differences across retail stores exist.
- Brainstorm what would happen if you introduced packaging types from premium locations to value locations, and vice versa. How would you need to adapt elements such as packaging type, size and price?
- Discuss how to address shopper needs that were previously unmet.
- Add a column to your Excel table describing the opportunity for growth and actions to carry out.

Outcome

Matrix with opportunities for pricing/packaging.

Case in point #1: Premium beers enter value channels

Around the globe, the number of beer breweries has ballooned, tapping into the desire for speciality craft beers. At the start, the craft brewers delivered to local restaurants and pubs, and they also started their own brewpubs. Slowly they found their way into the large, established grocery retailers. The speciality beers did not only appeal to shoppers but also to retailers who welcomed better margin products in a market where lager beer is often heavily discounted in promotion. As a result, Western markets have seen the number of beer products more than double over the past decade. On top of pressure on retail shelf, national beer brands experience higher demands for better terms from the retailers. As a result, they explored new channels and developed packaging solutions for discount grocery retail, specialist wholesalers and their own webstores.

Case in point #2: Discount furniture enters the professional market

Founded in 1918, Leen Bakker has a long heritage as a retailer of discount furniture and home decoration in the Benelux. They entered their discount proposition in the professional market, serving customer segments such as restaurants, holidays parks, real estate developers for short stay accommodation, offices and student housing. These clients buy the same consumer products but at a different price and in combination with customised services such as interior design, colour and style consultancy, transport and assembly.

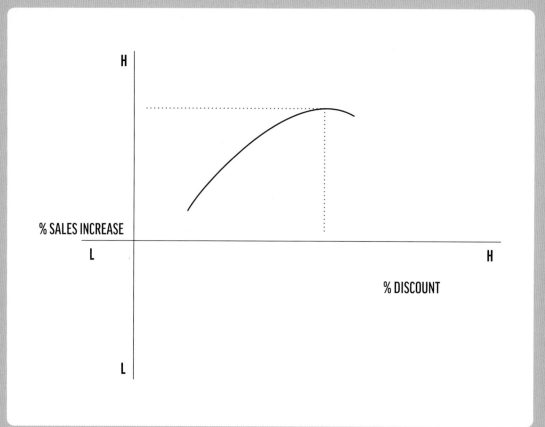

TOOL

How to find the optimal level of discount

User Group:	R & S
Challenge Level:	**
Time in Action Phase:	4 h

Situation

You want to increase the value perception of your promotions. More discount for the shopper leads to better value perception and sales uplift; however, there is a point at which the shopper starts to doubt the quality.

Goal

Finding a threshold discount percentage that is sufficiently attractive to shoppers and financially sound to run.

Preparation

- Create an experiment: Offer the same product in a display at five different levels of discount in five different stores - you may start at zero percent discount.
- Online stores run this experiment across groups of similar customers. For physical stores, ask permission to conduct an experiment in five stores during a week. Make sure stores are comparable and operate in similar catchment areas.
- This experiment is an alternative to more complex modelling so extra care should be given to identify any factors that create bias.
- For a base measurement: Compare sales versus same week last year and/or a comparable store.

Action

- Plot the outcomes of sales uplift for each discount percentage and draw a line between the dots.
- Identify percentage of discount when the sales increase is highest (see graph).
- You may replace sales by incremental sales, absolute margin or store traffic increase – depending on your promotion objective.
- Replace percentage of discount by absolute amount of discount, and see if product sales are sufficiently large to pay promotional fees to retailers.

Outcome

Chart indicating optimal discount level for next promotions.

Case in point #1: Total transparency when conducting experiments

In 2000, Amazon caused outrage among their customers when they found out that they had been subject to a pricing experiment. Amazon offered 68 DVDs at different price points to explore the optimal price level and price elasticity. In their apology, Amazon said they had randomly allocated customers to the various discount levels and refunded some 6.900 customers the difference between what they paid for a DVD and the lowest price paid. They promised that, if they conducted such an experiment again, they would automatically grant customers the lowest price after closure of the experiment.

Case in point #2: Close human watch on dynamic pricing

In June 2017, Uber's AI-enabled dynamic pricing system pushed up charges after the deadly terrorist attack in the London Bridge area. Surplus prices are a result of time of day, number of available Uber drivers and demand at a location. Uber disabled the surge pricing after some forty minutes in the immediate area of the attack. That human intervention remains necessary is illustrated by the fact that six months later Uber charged a Canadian rider 18,518.50 Canadian dollars (approx. €11.900) for a twenty-minute ride. Later a full refund was given for the ride.

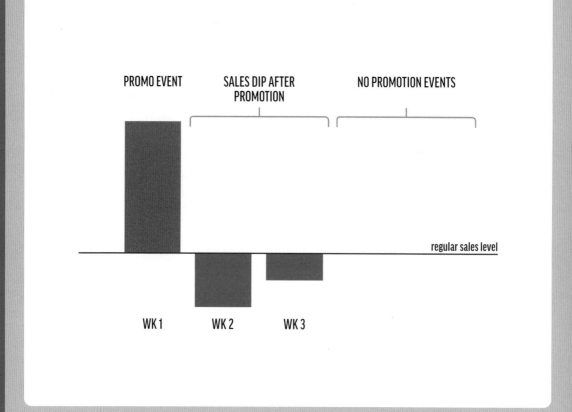

TOOL

5

How to decide on promotion frequency

User Group:	R & S
Challenge Level:	**
Time in Action Phase:	6 h

Situation

You would like to know how often a brand can be promoted. Promotions drive sales, however promotional frequency is lowered by factors such as number of competitor promotional slots and risk of loss of credibility of regular price. At a minimum, the sales uplift from the promotion should cover the negative effects from forward buying and pantry loading.

Goal

Determine the optimal frequency of promotions so that total sales are not hurt.

Preparation

- Obtain a list of promotional events by customer.
- Find out about the (ex-factory) sales by customer per week. Preferably also include data by product and/or brand.

Action

- Identify the regular (base) level of sales per week.
- Plot the sales difference versus regular level.
- After the promotion period, identify how many weeks lower sales levels persist for, compared to sales in a regular week.
- To determine the optimal interval between two promotional events, add two more weeks to the number of weeks of the sales dip (in red).
- Outcomes could be very different by product group, so calculate the net uplift by subtracting sales in period of sales dip (red) from sales uplift in the promotion period (grey).

Outcome

Number of promotional events by customer and product.

Case in point #1: Mark the next promotion on your calendar

Price and promotion comparison websites and social communities such as Reddit have made it very convenient for shoppers to track where they can find the best deal for a product. Shoppers share among themselves when large DIY retailers such as Lowe's and Home Depot give great deals ('every third week of the month' and 'around summer holidays and Labor Day') and which level of discount should be accepted ('wait for 40% off').

Case in point #2: Look at the effects of promotions from all angles

Retailers and suppliers often consider reducing the frequency of promotions. There are multiple reasons: during most promotions, the costs exceed the incremental sales; promotions are the largest cost factor after cost of goods; and they take up a lot of time – some 25% for a brand and account manager on supplier side, and 50% for a category manager. However, take the example of soft drinks. Suppliers know that a high frequency of promotions will block competitors from taking the promotional slot. A category manager in a grocery chain is interested in total category sales and promotional allowances paid by the brands. And the format manager sees that soft drinks promotions result in cross-sell of other categories. Therefore, all stakeholders need to be transparent on their objectives and work out an arrangement. For example, when agreeing that a specific brand is on promotion every other week, the costs of the promotional slots are agreed annually in advance and the category manager is rewarded on execution of the promotion rather than on category profits. Finally, the supplier and retailer can increase their understanding of promotion efficiency by combining their data sources and research methods.

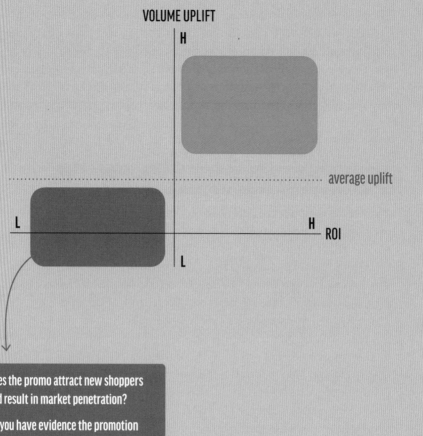

VOLUME UPLIFT

H

average uplift

L   H
                                          ROI
L

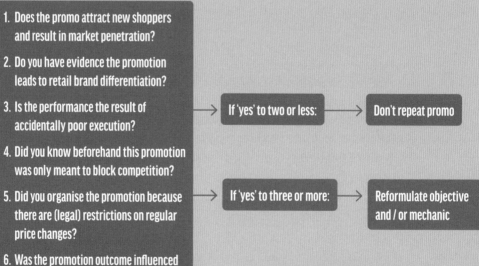

1. Does the promo attract new shoppers and result in market penetration?

2. Do you have evidence the promotion leads to retail brand differentiation?

3. Is the performance the result of accidentally poor execution?

4. Did you know beforehand this promotion was only meant to block competition?

5. Did you organise the promotion because there are (legal) restrictions on regular price changes?

6. Was the promotion outcome influenced by exceptional external conditions such as bad weather?

If 'yes' to two or less: → Don't repeat promo

If 'yes' to three or more: → Reformulate objective and / or mechanic

TOOL
6

How to improve promotional decision-making

User Group:	R & S
Challenge Level:	★★★
Time in Action Phase:	4 h

Situation

If you assume the absolute total promo spend is a given, could you allocate the same level of funds in better performing promotions? There always seems to be a good excuse not to invest resources in evaluation of promotions, though so much of our energy and budget are allocated here.

Goal

Allocate current promotional budget better.

Preparation

- Align what defines 'net profit' for ROI calculation. Try to include as many types of investments as possible, such as forward buying, discounts and advertising costs.
- Calculate the ROI and volume uplift of promotional events executed in the last twelve months.
- Gather a multifunctional team to discuss the promotions that are ranked either low or high.

Action

- Discuss the promotions with low ROI and low uplift. If they do not meet at least two out of six possible justifications provided in the list, do not repeat them.
- Discuss the promotions with high ROI/high uplift. What are success factors? Include these in your promotional manual and update each year.

Outcome

A set of approved promotional guidelines.

Case in point #1: End to deep price discounts

In 2016, Sainsbury's announced that they would be putting an end to BOGOF or Buy-One-Get-One-Free promotions, one of the most successful mechanisms in the UK grocery sector. Instead of steep deals, Sainsbury's invests in lower regular pricing levels. The decision was driven by the fact that shoppers had started to make more purchases but of a lower number of products. In addition, the majority of shoppers buy more than they actually need in multibuy and BOGOF promotions, while Sainsbury's aims to reduce food waste and the consumption of an excess of less healthy foods.

Case in point #2: Supplier reallocates promotional spend to permanently reduced prices

At the end of the previous century, P&G stopped price promotions and reinvested these in permanently reduced prices for the retailer and consumer. P&G said it found itself in a 'promotional zoo' in which brand equity of P&G brands were damaged, events often ran at a loss, the retail partners benefited more than they did, the events created frictions in the supply chain, and did not allow transparency of the real price. P&G thought promotions might work better for impulse products and not in categories that shoppers can stock. Not all promotion mechanisms were considered bad: direct marketing and sampling for new products were better than price-offs, multi-buys and on-pack promotions. Retailers did not welcome P&G's policy on what they saw as a way to rearrange their structure, an effective marketing instrument for all stakeholders and a way to compete on price with other grocers. Retailers reduced pricing of their private label to maintain price distance from the leading brands, which impacted retailer profits. The policy change might have come too late for shoppers as they had become used to promotions and considered them as inspirational diversions in their routine shopping trips. Even if shoppers say they prefer permanently lower prices more than promotions, their actions may speak differently.

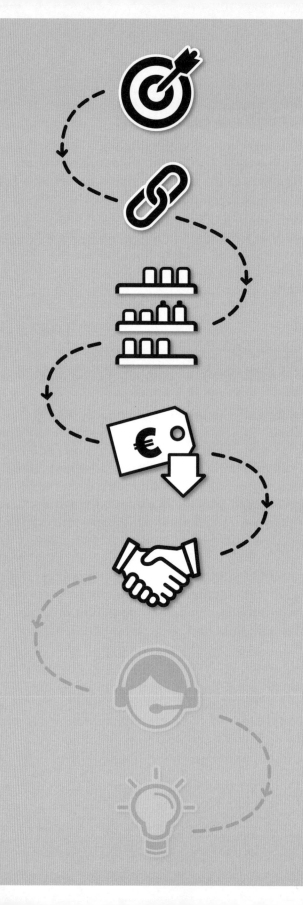

5 Leverage Category in Supplier – Retailer Relationship

TOOLS

1. How to prepare the conversation

2. How to structure the story

3. How to prioritise suppliers

4. How to prioritise retailers

5. How to create differentiated solutions for retailers

6. How to energise the collaboration

HAVE A MESSAGE – AUDIENCE – DELIVERY (OR SHORT: M.A.D.) – IDEA FOR CONVERSATION PREPARATION

Message

- What is the surprise? What is it that the audience does not know?
- What emotion would you like to leave them with?
- Can you sum up your message in two or three sentences?

Audience

- Who do you require to make a decision?
- What is the optimal order of approaching people?
- What is the best combination of people?
- What do you need to know about the individuals: Working style, Personality, Function, Ambition, Objectives?

Delivery

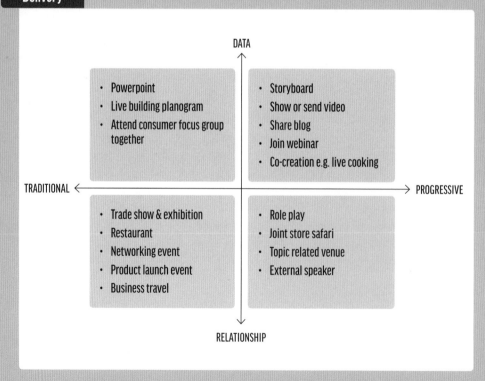

DATA

- Powerpoint
- Live building planogram
- Attend consumer focus group together

- Storyboard
- Show or send video
- Share blog
- Join webinar
- Co-creation e.g. live cooking

TRADITIONAL ← → PROGRESSIVE

- Trade show & exhibition
- Restaurant
- Networking event
- Product launch event
- Business travel

- Role play
- Joint store safari
- Topic related venue
- External speaker

RELATIONSHIP

TOOL

1

How to prepare the conversation

User Group:	S
Challenge Level:	**
Time in Action Phase:	6 h

Situation

You want to make meetings worthwhile and entertaining for everyone. A simple PowerPoint presentation may be all that is required to achieve the goals of the meeting. However, for special occasions or simply to grab the attention of Category Managers, a different approach is needed.

Goal

Choose the most effective way to deliver your message for your audience.

Preparation

- Define your message: Make a list of all the information you wish to convey and summarise the principal message in three sentences.
- Be deliberately focused on your audience: Obtain insights about the audience that you like to communicate with.
- Prepare for delivery: Choose the appropriate setting, taking into account the working style (traditional versus progressive) and focus of the conversation (data-driven versus relationship building) of all stakeholders.

Action

- Discuss or ask customers for their preferred working style.
- Determine the right mix of M.A.D.-ness: Message, Audience, Delivery for each conversation. Find ideas for ways of delivery in overview.
- Discuss which outcome you expect from each conversation and when (short- versus long-term).
- Create an annual calendar of messages and events.

Outcome

A M.A.D. approach that is varied and engaging based on a calendar of customer events for important supplier initiatives.

Case in point #1: Strategic objective taken seriously

Walmart not only seeks low prices from their suppliers, but they were also one of the first to develop more collaborative approaches. They drove the transition of customer manager roles at suppliers from terms negotiators to all-round business managers. When Walmart made a serious commitment to buy from suppliers that adhered to their sustainability monitoring system (called THESIS), this also impacted the daily responsibilities of customer managers. They had to answer Walmart's questions about environmental and social issues related to their products and deliver on improvements. During the implementation of the programme, each supplier meeting started with sustainability and the supplier's progress. In this way, Walmart reached the level of participation that they hoped for.

Case in point #2: Discovery meetings

Typically, supplier presentations contain too much detail for the retail customers, taking up precious time and losing out on relational aspects of engagements. Often, retailers consider the argumentation so fact-driven that it makes it almost impossible to have discussions on key category principles. When I was at PepsiCo, we decided to do things differently. We created a new customer engagement programme by training our customer and trade marketing people to conduct discovery meetings. These were meetings in which our customers spoke out first and no slides were used. It wasn't just about organising meetings, but also the follow-up. Depending on the customer objectives, we built fully customised shopper marketing campaigns or made adaptations to national programmes like 'Do us a flavour'.

7 STORYLINES

Fear
Identify the unseen threats and unexpected competitors.
How do we beat the monster?

Growth mindset
Highlight opportunities for growth.
What do we enjoy most and which goals motivate us intrinsically?

Reference
Show the journey of how to move from good to great.
Who is an aspirational benchmark?

Timeline
Show what has happened so far.
What have we learnt from the past and can we create lessons
for the future?

Crisis
Communicate action.
What are the most important actions to extinguish the fire?

Uncertainty
Give possible explanations of what happened, paint several
scenarios & give pros and cons.
What are the data and reliable sources?

Emotion
Relate what it means to the shopper in a sensory descriptive way
with rich detail.
How do we connect with shopper emotion?

TOOL

2

How to structure the story

User Group:	S
Challenge Level:	***
Time in Action Phase:	6 h

Situation

You want to spice up your story to keep your customer interested, even when there is less at stake, like in a sales update or minor product launch. Your delivery of the story influences how attentively retail customers listen and how much they look forward to your next visit. Of course, they are engaged if there is friction about pricing or expectations of large gains, but you want to create a positive impact at every opportunity.

Goal

Create an engaging and convincing story for supplier initiatives.

Preparation

- Write down the message you would like to convey to the retailer.
- Choose a delivery method (presentation, co-creation, etc.) that best fits you, the audience and the message.

Action

- Take a look at the seven storylines in the overview and select one that intuitively fits the occasion well.
- Take a couple of sheets of paper or large index cards. Experiment with the storyline by drafting a message on top and sketching a graph or image below. Make assumptions on what data research might tell.
- Try different storylines and decide which best delivers the message on the category.

Outcome

Draft storyline that forms structure for deeper data analysis and creative elaboration.

Case in point #1: Different storylines for a coffee brand launch

When Starbucks chose to extend their brand beyond cafés into the grocery channel, they could have chosen different storylines to persuade retailers to list them. Here are some examples of how to apply the seven storylines: 1) Impose their terms on the retailers by comparing themselves to other large coffee companies; 2) Show how growth in the grocery channel would rise from new occasions at home, as the Starbucks brand had so far been enjoyed only out-of-home; 3) Move from the launch in one coffee segment (e.g. ground coffee), to listings in all coffee segments and perhaps in-store coffee bars; 4) Demonstrate that incumbent brands had become so price elastic that the market had become too dependent on promotions and offer a way to counter that; 5) Signal the loss of shoppers to coffee shops in the past few years and offering a way to regain them; 6) Paint different scenarios of retailer engagement, from simple promotions to paying for signage and other merchandising for the brand in-store; 7) Show videos of how happy shoppers are when they find Starbucks in-store for the first time. Depending on the market conditions and the proactiveness of the category managers, the approach may vary. The important thing is to consider several options.

Case in point #2: How David can persuade Goliath

Food start-ups often combine passion and creativity to invent new products. Many build their brand reputation fast in their local community. Food start-ups that aim for nation-wide distribution need to address a number of aspects when they wish to deal with national grocery chains. To mention a few: 1) Evidence that their products are safe and production methods are at a high standard and have the right certification; 2) Packaging that is tested during all phases of the supply chain and communicates the product benefits in a salient manner on the retail shelf; 3) A business plan that shows in-depth consumer knowledge and scalable production and funding. It's really a matter of shifting perspective: large grocery retailers tend to sponsor food start-ups with advertising space and in line with market trends. However, they carefully watch whether the product is truly incremental to the category, helps differentiate the retailer brand and does not cannibalise their own labels. By integrating these aspects into the pitch around a great product, start-ups can persuade big distributors to join them in their quest for better food.

RETAILER DEPENDENCY ON SUPPLIER →

SUPPLIER DEPENDENCY ON RETAILER →

H

L ———————————————————————————— H

L

Enablers

IMAGE | PRIVATE LABEL

SUPPLIER 1

Partners

FINANCIAL | KNOWLEDGE

SUPPLIER 2

SUPPLIER 5

SUPPLIER 4

SUPPLIER 3

Transactional Supplier

OCCASIONAL | DEAL

Preferential Supplier

BIG BET | CUSTOMERS

Example:
Supplier 1 is very dependent on retailer, but the retailer can do without this supplier.

TOOL

3

How to prioritise suppliers

User Group:	R & S
Challenge Level:	***
Time in Action Phase:	4 h

Situation

You want to deepen the supplier-retailer relationship. The intensity and strength of the supplier-retailer relationship starts with an understanding of the mutual dependency.

Goal

Explore how much growth is still possible in developing the supplier-retailer relationship.

Preparation

- This exercise is designed for one retailer and one category.
- Make a list of all suppliers in the category at this retailer.
- Choose three to five factors to assess retailer dependency on each of these suppliers. Some factors are equal for all suppliers such as number of suppliers; some are different such as strength of A-brand. Give scores of one, two or three to each factor/supplier combination. Sum up all scores by supplier.
- Similarly, select three to five criteria for supplier dependency on retailer such as percentage of sales at the retailer and category entry barriers. Again, give scores of one, two or three to each factor/supplier combination and sum up.

Action

- Draw a horizontal axis to represent retailer dependency on suppliers and plot supplier dependency on the vertical axis. Optional: display category growth or supplier sales as size of the bubble.
- After calculating average scores there are four quadrants. In the top right quadrant, suppliers are very dependent on the retailer and vice versa, which makes them 'partners'. The reason for the position in the quadrant is either positive (red) or negative (grey). So, the top right partner score might be the outcome of unique knowledge or purely financially driven. Design strategies to maintain position if desired, or amend if risky.

Outcome

Assessment of strength/vulnerability of supplier-retailer relationships.

Case in point #1: Continuous onboarding of suppliers

The grocery chain H-E-B is proud of its Texan roots, which is reflected in the way they work with both their customers and suppliers. On the H-E-B website, suppliers obtain easy access to a range of documents, tools and systems that allow them to keep track of the processes of product maintenance, ordering and payments throughout the supply life cycle. They help suppliers onboard by clarifying in simple terms the requirements of doing business, for example with regard to food safety, and encourage them to seek assistance when needed. As they say at H-E-B: 'When we move into a neighborhood, we strive to provide much more than food. We're in the people business. We just happen to sell groceries.' Their programme to include locally owned small food and beverage suppliers is one of the ways to make this happen. Furthermore, through their supplier diversity programme, they look for suppliers owned and operated by minorities.

Case in point #2: Integrated versus specialist suppliers

Over the last decade, the Spanish grocer Mercadona has adapted their supplier policy for private label products. First, Mercadona replaced the traditional negotiation model by integrated collaboration based on contracts of an infinite time period. Some 120 suppliers produced all or most products within a category. If one of the parties wanted to end the relationship, they needed to take into account a three-year waiting period. Most of these suppliers were 80% or more dependent on their sales to Mercadona. This way of working ensured stability but gave little opportunity for suppliers to seek new business opportunities and for Mercadona to develop the category. Therefore, Mercadona also started working with some 1.300 specialist suppliers for a limited range of products. To increase speed of innovation while keeping costs low, Mercadona gave a new twist to the supplier model: for new products, both integrated and specialist suppliers were invited to submit their concepts.

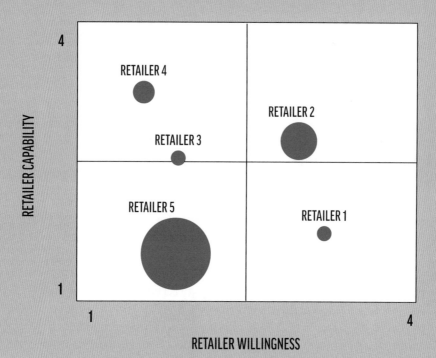

TOOL

How to prioritise retailers

User Group:	S
Challenge Level:	**
Time in Action Phase:	2 h

Situation

As a supplier you want to carefully select the retail customers you form tight relationships with because ideas for category development only truly become ideas after implementation in a store. Suppliers may find out that their largest, most sophisticated retail customer is not the most suitable partner for their category growth initiatives.

Goal

Prioritise your retail customers to work on category growth initiatives.

Preparation

- Collect sales data of your top retail customers for the past year (covering > 80% of supplier sales).
- Send out a survey to your sales and shopper marketing teams to assess willingness of retailer to collaborate with you as a supplier (scale one to four).
- Define criteria of retailer capability of category management such as retailer openness to data sharing, opportunities to test new ideas, discipline to execute according to agreed plan.
- Assess capability of retailers on these criteria.

Action

- Plot willingness and capability on axes of graph as shown, and let the size of the bubble reflect the size of retailer sales.
- In your team, discuss which initiatives build the category and fit the top retailers.
- Decide which retailer to contact first: the most capable, the most willing, or the largest?

Outcome

Alignment on best partners for category growth.

Case in point #1: New prioritisation after increased market concentration

In 2018, Tesco and Carrefour, who both rank in the top 10 of global grocery retailers, announced that they would partner in sourcing international A-brands, private label products and not-for-resale goods. The alliance had different implications for each of the supplier types. The international A-brand suppliers feared a deterioration of their negotiation position and pricing. Small suppliers saw new opportunities because Tesco thought they were more agile and had out-innovated the big firms. Increasingly, the large suppliers have explored other ways of distribution such as direct-to-consumer delivery. Tesco private label suppliers saw new business opportunities as the potential for growth with Tesco is small as compared to Carrefour (half of Tesco sales already come from private labels versus a third at Carrefour). Carrefour private label suppliers and not-for-resale suppliers may have deprioritised working with the new alliance as a result of the increased risk of losing business.

Case in point #2: Focus resources on largest customers

At the end of the eighties, P&G was known for their transactional, adversarial relationships with retail customers in the United States. A couple of insights made them realise they were on the wrong track. First of all, they achieved a lower share with large customers such as Walmart than might be expected based on the national P&G share. Secondly, large customers might be larger than country organisations though they would be supported by up to fifteen times fewer employees. Thirdly, P&G leadership realised that though their brands pulled shopper traffic to retail stores, P&G was more expensive and more inflexible than other suppliers. P&G changed their mission towards building long-term relationships, open communication on category performance measures and multi-functional customer teams focusing on their largest retail customers. Prices for retailers decreased as a result of the exchange of information among partners and a more holistic view of the supply chain. Thanks to this change in approach, P&G saw their market share increase in most of their categories.

RETAILER STRATEGY	SOCIETY TRENDS
Objectives	Mood
Target Group	Trends
Brand Positioning	Seasons

SHOPPER INSIGHTS	COMPETITION
Issues	Strengths
Message In-store	Communication
Emotions	Target Group

Examples with increasing level of engagement

SUPPLIER BRAND

PRODUCT	One product exclusive for three months →	Some products of supplier brand are permanently exclusive
PROMOTION	Tailor-made graphic on display →	Shopper marketing campaign
PRICE	Amend packaging size for better pricing →	Develop value brand for category
PLACE	Support with field sales force →	All products have different distribution per store (cluster)

TOOL

5

How to create differentiated solutions for retailers

User Group:	R & S
Challenge Level:	***
Time in Action Phase:	4 h

Situation

Retailers prefer strong brands for bringing in traffic to their stores. However, if supplier brands have national distribution, the retail brand cannot differentiate itself just on the basis of listing this brand. Therefore, suppliers and retailers are encouraged to find other ways to work with the supplier brand and still deliver retailer differentiation.

Goal

Support the retail brand by delivering a retailer specific initiative.

Preparation

- Collect trends and information from four perspectives (see overview):
  - Retailer strategy, e.g. is the retail brand about service? Does the main target group consist of millennials?
  - Society trends, e.g. can the category play a role in the back-to-school season?
  - Shopper insights, e.g. what are emotional moments when shopping the category?
  - Competition, e.g. which segments in the category are not addressed in competitive retailer advertising?

Action

- In the preparation phase, you researched all areas relevant for retail brand. Next, select an area and brainstorm how this could be activated through the supplier marketing mix: product, promotion, price, place.
- The examples in the overview show that the level of engagement by the retailer may vary. This depends on the level of trust and strategic partnership between supplier and retailer.
- The preparation and action phases are ideally conducted in the form of a joint exploration by retailer and supplier.

Outcome

An area of collaboration between supplier and retailer that drives category sales.

Case in point #1: Leverage festive moments for different product packaging and price points

The chocolate brand Ferrero Rocher delivers different offers to retailers while the core product remains the same. They do so by varying the product packaging. Often, they tap into the emotional gifting and festive moments of the year. For example, at Christmas time Ferrero Rocher was available in six formats of different sizes and packaging types at the Belgian Carrefour hypermarkets; one of them was called 'The golden experience', with six pieces. Colruyt supermarkets also offered six formats, but only two of them coincided with the Carrefour offer (though at a lower price at Colruyt). The so-called collection box was offered in a format of 24 pieces at Carrefour while Colruyt offered the same chocolates in boxes of 15 and 32 pieces. Through packaging variation, the price per gram of chocolate could vary among the packaging formats for essentially the same product.

Case in point #2: Differentiating by retailer and by season allows for customised combinations

Conagra Brands is uniquely positioned to customise their approach to retail customers and to help retailers differentiate. First of all, they manage dozens of iconic U.S. brands that they can carefully match with the retailer strategy and the retailers' shopper target groups. Also, Conagra Brands has built a good reputation for their shopper marketing campaigns. For example, through one-to-one interviews across the country, Conagra Brands identified six seasons among grocery shoppers (Post-Holiday, Spring, Summer, Back to School, October Fling and Holiday). When addressing the shopper needs in each of the seasons, they made sure they customised the campaign by retailer. In order to drive conversations with customers and to obtain shopper insights on a continuous basis, Conagra has built a suite of tools to drive customised analyses and set up multifunctional teams close to customer headquarters.

3 X S-MODEL

Stores

BOTTOM THREE STORES	TOP THREE STORES
▪ _____	▪ _____
▪ _____	▪ _____
▪ _____	▪ _____

IDEA
- ▪ Visit the bottom three stores and top three stores together.
- ▪ Take photos. Compare.
- ▪ Find root causes.

Staff

IDEA
- ▪ Jointly visit staff in stores and interview.
- ▪ And for office staff: Shadow your counterpart for half a day.

Shoppers

THREE SURVEYS AMONG SHOPPERS, SUPPLIER, RETAILER

TOPICS
- ▪ Sustainability
- ▪ In-store experience
- ▪ Website navigation
- ▪ Staff friendliness etc.

IDEA
- ▪ Conduct online surveys and/or in-store interviews and compare views of Shoppers, Supplier and Retailer on same topic.

TOOL

6

How to energise the collaboration

User Group:	R & S
Challenge Level:	**
Time in Action Phase:	4 d

Situation

You want to generate new insights by finding fresh perspectives together and breaking patterns of engagement. Sometimes suppliers and retailers rely so much on the performance indicators in their standard reports that they forget to explore explanations of success and failure in a fresh, pragmatic manner. Deviation from the regularly scheduled meeting may help create new positive energy.

Goal

Stimulate retailer-supplier collaboration by discovering insights together.

Preparation

- In the action phase, supplier and retailer spend three days together to collect insights from three perspectives: Stores, Staff, Shoppers, therefore exercises for these days need to be prepared. Examples of exercises are offered in the overview.
- Make sure you appoint joint supplier and retailer teams. If there is time pressure, people could choose from the three days.
- Option: Frame the exercises around an important category challenge to give more direction to the insights discovery.

Action

- Work in pairs (one person from supplier, one from retailer) during the three days.
- On the fourth day, everyone presents the main findings to one another.
- Find explanations for what happened.
- Identify how perspectives from Stores x Staff x Shoppers result in more category Sales.

Outcome

More understanding between organisations and ideas for category development.

Case in point #1: Creative customer meetings delivering inspiration

The most effective energisers for better collaboration between retailer and supplier also generate insights into the category. My favourite top three examples are: 1) A beer manufacturer that took board members to the homes of people of low income to see for themselves the role beer and alcohol play in their lives; 2) A food company that let team members put on a sort of sumo suit, special gloves and glasses to experience how seniors open their food packaging; 3) A beverages supplier that invited a retailer to a meeting in which actors carrying bags and shopping lists demonstrated the in-store shopping experience. Not all supplier-retailer relationships are ready for this type of meet-up but if they do, they make a great story and a special memory among the participants.

Case in point #2: Wizard of Oz partnership in e-commerce

Wizard of Oz is a methodology often used in digital product development, in which the team pretends as if the product is already available online. One of the most famous examples is Zappos, as their founder actually validated his business idea using the Wizard of Oz. He took photos of actual shoes in shoe stores, offered them online and if a purchase was made he would return to the store, buy the shoes and ship them to the client. From the client's perspective, this seemed to be an automated task but in reality it was a validation that people wanted to buy shoes online, even though at that time it was assumed they wouldn't. These days people will purchase almost everything online, and a methodology like the Wizard of Oz is an excellent way to energise collaboration and offer suppliers the opportunity to do soft launches of new products, in order to learn together what works best and what the market is ready for.

6 Build Services for Category Engagement

TOOLS

1. How to improve the experience of the shopping trip

2. How to identify cues for new services

3. How to discern whether shoppers enjoy time spent

4. How to identify friction and triggers in the shopping tasks

5. How to create ideas for a new store concept

6. How to revisit shopper expectations

	Planning	Shopping	Consuming
What do you see the shopper doing?			
What does the shopper feel? (+)			
(-/-)			
Which behaviour do you want to influence in which manner?			

TOOL

How to improve the experience of the shopping trip

User Group:	R & S
Challenge Level:	****
Time in Action Phase:	1 d

Situation

As a supplier, you can say many good things about your product, but you are wondering which benefit resonates best at each point during the shopping trip. As a retailer, you are wondering if there are possible improvements for shopper interaction.

Goal

Find inspiration to remove shopping pain points and/or deliver shopper delight.

Preparation

- During the action phase, you follow people during shopping. If you want to ask them to buy from a certain category, pre-recruitment of shoppers is required. If a specific purchase is not required, you could observe shoppers at a greater distance, which has the benefit of more natural shopping behaviour.
- Select store or prepare online tracking tool.
- Prepare cards with a number of different smileys (from distressed to happy).

Action

- Observe the behaviour of +/- ten shoppers and write down what they do.
- If they are pre-recruited, prompt the shopper at several intervals to circle the smiley that reflects their emotions. If you intercept shoppers only at the end of the shopping trip, you rely on them to remember how they felt during different stages of the trip. Place the smileys above and below the line reflecting how negative or positive these were.
- After completing the observation, together with the shopper reflect on what could provide a solution to any issue.
- Summarise the +/- ten trips into one overview.

Outcome

Qualitative input for better approaches to engaging with the shopper.

Case in point #1: Traffic generation through influencers

Shoppers often feel overwhelmed by the number of brands and styles available, and besides, how do they know the fashion will fit their personal style? This is why they rely on friends and influencers on Instagram and other social media. Once they feel comfortable with the style of an influencer, the curated assortment makes shopping more pleasant. In turn, fashion retailers work with influencers to promote their brands in reviews on social media. This is why we are seeing a rise in influencer platforms such as RewardStyle that select influencers that fit certain brands and develop campaigns. This leads shoppers to the moment of purchase. Once shoppers are in the (online) store, fashion retailers must take the lead again by creating a strong experience that confirms the choice and enhances the influencer's reach; for example, through the use of special discount codes, hashtags, use of referral marketing and even exclusive items or limited edition collections developed together with the influencers.

Case in point #2: Shopper arguments change over time

Noting that shoppers no longer bought their washing machine at specialised appliance-sellers but at multi-category online stores, the Miele brand needed to work harder to be considered by shoppers. New selling arguments were required to bring light to this German brand that is known for quality, because the traditional distributors sold in a product-oriented manner, mostly talking about capacity and longevity. In order to capture the diversity of online searches, Miele started communicating from a shopper perspective; for example, the need for a small, quick wash and the concern for maintaining the quality of the fabrics. And of course, shopper criteria will continue to change and evolve. Increasingly shoppers seek benefits such as keeping the noise down in busy cities and saving both the planet and their money by buying energy and water efficient machines. These are more meaningful purchase criteria than product features such as soap sensors or smartphone operated washing machines.

TOOL

2

How to identify cues for new services

User Group:	R & S
Challenge Level:	***
Time in Action Phase:	1 d

Situation

You want to look for ways to improve the shopper experience. When services on top of the physical product are essential for shopper satisfaction, such as for fashion or fresh groceries categories, small changes in how and when you interact could make a big difference in the way the total product is perceived.

Goal

Test different scenarios in order to improve shopper satisfaction with services.

Preparation

- Simulate a shopping environment where the shopper receives the service (home for online store). Use attributes or props like on a film set or theatre to make it feel real. Prepare to engage in role-play.
- Prepare several scenarios about which you want to know the impact, such as an angry shopper or low light.
- Work with a minimum of three people.

Action

- Assign and rotate three roles among your team: Shopper, Service provider, Observer.
- After each scenario, discuss what you observed, thought, and felt.
- Come up with ideas on what might improve the service, replay the scenario introducing these ideas, then evaluate the improved outcome. Select the ones that make a difference.

Outcome

Ideas for delivering better service to shoppers.

Case in point #1: Reimagine the needs of your customers

Primark stores are known for high densities of both merchandise and shoppers resulting in the discount fashion image the retail brand seeks to establish. Recently, Primark opened a store in Birmingham (UK) surprising their customers with new services. For example, an in-store beauty salon offers manicures, pedicures and facial treatments, and shoppers can get a haircut at the barbershop. To cater to families with children, it also opened a Disney-themed café. More related to their core categories of clothing and accessories is the 'Snap and Share' room where shoppers share pictures of the clothes they try on, while setting the scene with the music and lighting they like.

Case in point #2: Staff plays service scenarios

Role-play helped invent fast food service. At traditional drive-in restaurants in the fifties, waitresses took the orders at the car, and more often than the customer liked, returned late or with the wrong burger. The McDonald brothers set out to increase the speed of service. They chalked out the layout of the kitchen on an empty tennis court and asked their staff to simulate the preparation of meals. The brothers kept changing the arrangements of kitchen appliances till they could promise the fulfilment of an order within 30 seconds. The layout of the kitchen and all other aspects of the first restaurants were only focused on speeding up the service to the shoppers: staff specialised in specific tasks to increase efficiency, the composition of the burger was fixed, and the menu was kept small.

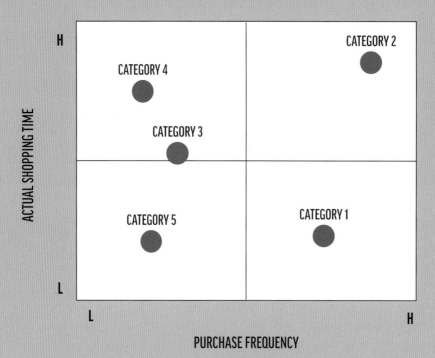

TOOL

3

How to discern whether shoppers enjoy time spent

User Group:	R & S
Challenge Level:	***
Time in Action Phase:	2 d

Situation

You wonder how your shoppers perceive the time spent shopping your category. There are plenty of statistics that show high correlation between the number of items purchased (sales) and the time spent (duration of shopping trip), but each time one needs to determine the cause and the result. While some believe that longer shopping times are good for sales, others believe the shopping trip should be as fast and convenient as possible. Yet the shopper's perception is what matters most. In addition, by comparing the time spent with that for other categories, suppliers and retailers, you obtain clues for improved merchandising.

Goal

Identify categories where shoppers spend more (or less) time than they actually like.

Preparation

- Ask permission to observe and survey some forty shoppers in-store.
- Apart from your category, select at least four other categories.

Action

- Observe how much time shoppers actually spend shopping the category. Use a timer and make notes.
- At the end, ask shoppers how often they buy the category, and to what degree they are satisfied with the shopping trip.
- Plot the actual shopping time against purchase frequency. One would expect shopping time to decrease with higher purchase frequency. Investigate categories that deviate from this expectation by checking perceived waiting time and shopper satisfaction score. In fact, no further action is urgent if perceived waiting time is low and shopper satisfaction is high.

Outcome

Cues for changes in size and composition of assortment and merchandising to align with time spent in category.

Case in point #1: Measure engagement through own app

Rather than using time as a measure, a Burberry store in Shenzhen monitors engagement with the help of a customised WeChat app. In fact, the shopper data comes in before the visit, because the majority of the customer journeys for luxury goods in China start digitally; for example, by searching exclusive content or making an in-store appointment, which can be done through the app. Within the store, shoppers are followed through their QR code scans. By scanning the QR codes attached to the Burberry product, they can see models showing the item and other exclusive content. Each shopper action is rewarded by app-related currency, which allows shoppers to pay for food and drinks in the café but also for characters and clothing for their characters in the app.

Case in point #2: Delivering experiences to enhance transactions

For some categories and trips, shoppers enjoy spending time at the store. It becomes an immersive experience rather than just a transactional visit. Take Under Armour's flagship store in Chicago, which contains all kinds of elements that make you stay longer: a large bust to make Instagrammable pictures, a trampoline to measure and display how high a person jumps, a bar (not just a department) for wearables and an impressive living wall. While the time spent in-store by shoppers is high, the actual sales are driven by increased traffic thanks to the experience as they are drawn to the large assortment on two floors. Tailoring the experience to the shopper is key. Other retailers benefit from ultrafast services and achieve high sales per minute. For example, they facilitate the click and collect experience and give a high sense of service as the products wait for you. U.S. drugstores Walgreens and CVS promote the use of their apps so that people buy prescription medicines and photo development online and pick up these in-store or at the curbside (BOPIS or Buy Online Pick up In-Store).

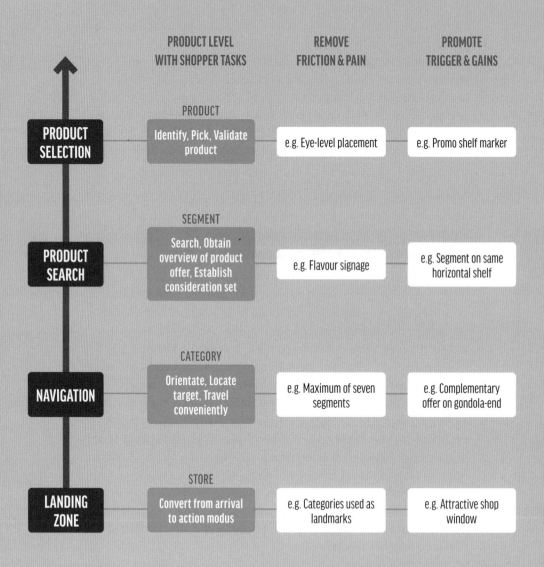

	PRODUCT LEVEL WITH SHOPPER TASKS	REMOVE FRICTION & PAIN	PROMOTE TRIGGER & GAINS
PRODUCT SELECTION	PRODUCT Identify, Pick, Validate product	e.g. Eye-level placement	e.g. Promo shelf marker
PRODUCT SEARCH	SEGMENT Search, Obtain overview of product offer, Establish consideration set	e.g. Flavour signage	e.g. Segment on same horizontal shelf
NAVIGATION	CATEGORY Orientate, Locate target, Travel conveniently	e.g. Maximum of seven segments	e.g. Complementary offer on gondola-end
LANDING ZONE	STORE Convert from arrival to action modus	e.g. Categories used as landmarks	e.g. Attractive shop window

TOOL

4

How to identify friction and triggers in the shopping tasks

User Group:	R & S
Challenge Level:	***
Time in Action Phase:	1 d

Situation

A friction is anything that slows down, annoys or hinders the shopping task completely. Though it is fantasy to think that the 100% frictionless shopping journey will ever exist and that technology should always replace human engagement, it is better to chop the shopping tasks into slices and meet the friction head-on. You want to better understand the shopping task, breaking it down into more detail to see how you might improve it. In highly competitive markets, even the smallest friction may divert the shoppers' attention away from making the sales. Thus, professionals need to build a checklist of possible friction and trigger points. Making the shopping tasks explicit helps discover areas of improvement.

Goal

Increase understanding of the different phases of a shopping task, and where changes should be made to please the shopper.

Preparation

- Make a shopping list with products from three different categories. This shopping list will be used during the action phase and the selected categories enable inspiration for comparison on best practice merchandising.
- Gather a team from different functions.

Action

- Work in pairs: one shops and one observes.
- After completion of the trip, get together and group your observations into the four levels of the shopping trip (see overview). Discuss what happened in each phase. The observer asks How & Why, and together you identify what motivated and what stopped the shopper.
- Rotate teams, exchange roles and conduct one more shopping trip.
- Analyse the findings to see where improvement has been achieved that can be implemented.

Outcome

Inspiration to improve shopping experience clustered around four groups of shopping tasks.

Case in point #1: Accompany the shopping journey with relevant tools along the way

Soon after landing on the websites of Zalando or Macy's, shoppers navigate to the desired category with the help of filters and clickable images related to the time of the year or perhaps linked to their previous visits. Product pages often include social sharing buttons. However, retailers have come to realise that these are not often used. The social sharing button may distract shoppers from browsing products and actually clutter the page. And if the number of shares next to the button is low, shoppers perceive the product as less attractive. The lesson here is that you need to accompany the needs as they evolve during the journey. Shoppers may not be ready for social sharing when they are still deciding, but at that stage they might actually want to check out reviews. So retailers should focus on selling first, and only after the sale, allow for sharing on social media. Retailers may also conduct research on which of their shoppers see sharing as important, and which shoppers focus their visit to the website on taking in content and buying products. Tailoring the journey to those needs helps to avoid dropout, navigation away from the page and shopping cart abandonment.

Case in point #2: Digital makes searching, ordering and paying really easy

Eating a Chipotle burrito is delicious, but waiting for one is terrible. Therefore, Chipotle makes ordering as convenient as possible, starting with the website, which mentions free delivery in bold letters so there is little chance of an abandoned bag at checkout. The Chipotle app is very flexible in letting you choose between delivery and pick-up, selecting a pick-up time or even reserving a future pick-up time, and when shoppers start an order they can share a link with someone else who can then add to the same order. If you forget to scan your app for your loyalty points, you can always come back later to scan your receipt. The added advantage is that the digital footprint informs the Chipotle team of further potential improvements to make the experience even better.

TOOL

5

How to create ideas for a new store concept

User Group:	R
Challenge Level:	****
Time in Action Phase:	1 d

Situation

You want to create a new store that meets the expectations of all stakeholders as harmoniously as possible. When building a new store concept, people soon realise that the objectives and interests of the various retail functions may collide or diverge. People are aware of this but do not always express their opinions or do so only late in the process. By designing a playful and relaxed environment, this could be addressed.

Goal

Obtain clarity on the objectives and interests of all relevant retail functions early in the process of store design.

Preparation

- Describe a new store concept and provide guidelines such as size of assortment and primary shopper target group.
- Each department, such as Concept Development, Store Operations and Finance, prepares objectives, KPIs and trends. These are summarised on one or two A4 pages and brought into the action phase exercise.
- Gather eight to twelve people from different departments.

Action

- The facilitator introduces the store concept challenge.
- First, people build the store concept with Lego blocks and figures within their functional silos.
- Each team presents their scale model. On a flipchart, the facilitator writes where the models are equal, and where they diverge.
- Option: In a second round, the Lego store is built by multifunctional teams.
- At the end of the exercise, get clarity on common ground and areas that need further discussion.

Outcome

A simple model of your new store concept with a better understanding of conflicting interests and objectives in the design process.

Case in point #1: Involve the local community

To best fulfil the needs of local neighbourhoods, Walmart has reinvigorated their store for the community programme. For the development of new services in their Neighbourhood Markets format, they involved store management to create locally relevant solutions. As a result, a new Bentonville store included a pastry counter supplied by a local, well-known bakery. Local involvement is becoming increasingly important because of climate change, sustainability and conscious consumerism. An example of how this affects retail formats is the UK initiative 'The People's Supermarket' and their 'The People's Kitchen' which aim for a healthier and more sustainable model. Products are local, team members are neighbours, produce is fresh and seasonal. Their success is not in their scale, but in the high involvement – and, ultimately, preference – of their community.

Case in point #2: Pressure from competing channels drives overhaul of store concept

Though 85% of office supplies are sold offline in the U.S., shoppers are increasingly migrating to the online channel. Brick-and-mortar stores of Office Depot face competition from specialised webstores, from online giant Amazon and from electronics retailers. To better understand shopping behaviour, Office Depot conducted interviews with shoppers, shadowed how they made their purchases, and built a pilot store at their head offices. This led to recommendations to improve navigation through the lower shelves, removal of signs and category signage. The revised strategy has led to a reallocation of space, and product groups serving the same needs were brought together. As a result of the shift to online purchasing, Office Depot has reduced their number of outlets. Also, they have shifted the sales mix from the traditional product categories such as paper and ink cartridges to office furniture, cleaning products and copy and print services. As part of an agreement with Alibaba, the stores will provide their U.S. customers with fulfilment services for purchases made at Alibaba.com. And for business customers, more space is devoted to the business support centre, which delivers all kinds of services to small and medium-sized companies such as printing, shipping and technology support.

	EXAMPLE
Define shopper issue	Long queues at checkout

WHERE CAN YOU FIND THIS ATTRIBUTE?

Which industries / objects have high 'speed of service'? What is the purpose & benefit?	Examples are F1, emergency room, Twitter, McDonald's
Which industries have low 'speed of service'? What is the purpose & benefit?	Examples are civil service, turtle, 5-star restaurant, slowfood

ASK YOURSELF: WHAT IF YOU ...

exaggerate?	Introduce F1 pitstop
change order?	Pay upfront
eliminate steps / ingredients?	Reduce assortment by 50%
reframe as a benefit?	Enjoy TV & friendly staff at checkout
double the price?	Premium store
reduce costs by 50%?	Self-scan

TOOL

6

How to revisit shopper expectations

User Group:	R & S
Challenge Level:	****
Time in Action Phase:	4 h

Situation

You want to unclutter your offering and make sure it is aligned with the needs of the market. Initially, when the store opened, service was simple and straightforward. However, over time more products are introduced, direct communication with the shopper halts and cost-reduction measures drive out personalisation. The challenge is that you overlook changes in shoppers' preferences.

Goal

Critically assess whether the service that is provided for a specific category or for the complete shopping trip is still aligned with what shoppers expect today.

Preparation

- Prepare a relaxed environment for meeting up in the action phase.
- Send a quick communication to participants informing them that the creative session aims for actualisation, and briefing them to prepare by looking at trends, competitor offering, and their own preferences these days.
- Find a group energiser or warm-up that you can use in the action phase; for example, at sessionlab.com.

Action

- Get the creative juices flowing with energisers.
- Take fifteen minutes to brainstorm about shopper issues that require a solution.
- Select a shopper issue; start thinking about how other sectors address this issue. Ask the questions you find in the overview and start building different scenarios for the store.
- Once you have identified all the issues and brainstormed them, select the most promising initiatives and rank them according to speed of implementation and degree of market alignment. Create a road map with the best initiatives.

Outcome

A road map of ideas on how you could improve shopper experience (for a specific category purchase).

Case in point #1: Shopper benefit beyond physical product

Up to 1973, speed of delivery had not been a major shopper decision factor. Then Domino's Pizza redefined the pizza category by refocusing from the physical product to the shopping experience. The key benefit became speed, while continuing to maintain the quality standards of their brand. They promised to deliver warm pizzas to your home in thirty minutes or you would receive a pizza for free. Differentiating on speed directly impacted the operations in the kitchen, work and transport means of deliverers, as well as ingredients from suppliers. And in so doing, Domino's changed the category standard by shifting the shopper expectations for any other pizza delivery service.

Case in point #2: Lidl manages expectations for fruit and vegetables

For a long time, Lidl suffered from a poor image of their fruit and vegetables in the Netherlands. This started to change when Lidl redefined their market from hard discount shopping to grocery shopping. It no longer wanted to depend on low prices and non-food promotions for driving traffic. Instead, fresh products should drive multiple visits per week. When expanding their fruit and vegetable department, they carefully chose other grocery stores as their benchmark, as they knew they would never be able to compete with greengrocers in terms of size of assortment, store ambience and staff expertise. Lidl created a strong perception of quality in their fruit and vegetable department by 1) leveraging the insight that shoppers base their perception of fruit and vegetable quality on some five types only; 2) restricting the assortment size to fast rotating items that have less chance to turn to waste; 3) creating a spacious ambience and therefore the perception of better quality compared to dry grocery categories; 4) organising consumer campaigns such as street colouring of vegetables and vegetable-shaped plush giveaways; 5) leveraging the fact that shoppers have higher expectations on quality from service grocery stores than from Lidl. The investments in fruit and vegetables have resulted in more visits and a halo effect in the perception of quality from fruit and vegetables to other categories.

7   Innovate Your Category

TOOLS

1. How to phrase shopper arguments
2. How to identify the source of incrementality
3. How to select the best category initiatives
4. How to scope for innovation
5. How to boost the value of a small basket
6. How to bundle new brand ideas into category themes

REVOLUTIONARY & NEW

LINK
- Show or explain the connection between the new product and the user context.
- Help the user assimilate by using System 1 heuristics such as framing.

PROVE
- Prove through logical argumentation and clear examples that consuming the new product is a wise, sensible decision.
- Be clear by highlighting features and functions that explain in System 2 terms how this product is a tangible improvement on the current offerings.

LOW INVOLVEMENT & DISCONNECTED

HIGH INVOLVEMENT & RELEVANT

COMPARE
- Focus on the improvement and praise what is different and its effect on the user context.
- Create clear references, reviews or testimonials by using System 1 heuristics such as topic experts and a feeling of status.

DEMONSTRATE
- Provide compelling, rational argumentation on the differences and improvements.
- Summarise clear System 2 arguments and analytics as supporting evidence.

FAMILIAR BUT BETTER

TOOL

How to phrase shopper arguments

User Group:	**R & S**
Challenge Level:	***
Time in Action Phase:	**4 h**

Situation

As retailer or supplier, you can think of 1.000 reasons why a (new) product offers benefits for the shopper, but it is difficult to identify which argument works best. Sometimes you need to apply rational argumentation in your communication; at other times, tapping into emotions is more effective.

Goal

Find a compelling argument for a shopper to purchase a product, which could be existing or new, and is low or high involvement.

Preparation

- During the preparation phase, construct a survey:
  - Build a survey whereby participants score one or more products on a scale of one to ten on the degree of novelty (familiar versus revolutionary new), and the degree of involvement (disconnected versus highly relevant).
  - Each product is shown in a similar manner: short concept description with the option of product image.
  - Distribute the survey to people outside your organisation. Try to reach one hundred people – a representative sample of your shoppers.
- Optionally, to better understand the difference between an automatic shopper response and emotional bias (System 1 thinking) versus deliberate response and rational consideration (System 2 thinking), you may want to familiarise yourself with Daniel Kahneman's book, *Thinking, Fast and Slow*.

Action

- Plot the outcomes of the survey as shown. The axes are based on the average of product scores. Alternatively assume a score of five as a perceived middle score.
- Apply the guidelines from the model to select and sharpen your communication on the product to the shopper.

Outcome

Clearly categorised actionable list of product argumentation.

Case in point #1: Get heard in the beauty market with a new skincare brand

Getting heard as a beauty brand is hard; convincing people to scrub coffee leftovers on their body to make them feel better is even more challenging. This is what a former Australian coffee store owner did when he started the skincare brand Frank Body. He emphasised the good things inside coffee and other ingredients but didn't use rational, scientific arguments and corporate jargon. Instead, the brand created a character, Frank, who communicates with shoppers in a first-person, cheeky and humorous manner when promoting products: 'My blend of coffee, vitamin E, and antioxidant-rich oils keep your skin looking perky, even and soft. Enough introductions. Time to get naked.' They promote the sharing of user reviews and referrals through their loyalty programme, Pink Hotel, which rewards engagement better at each level: the lobby, pool deck, junior suite and penthouse.

Case in point #2: Stick to the brand promise but deliver it in a modern way

Millennials had stopped buying Häagen-Dazs ice cream because they no longer recognised themselves in the advertisements. While keeping the brand positioning of luxurious moments of indulgence for adults, Häagen-Dazs sought to bring the message in a more inclusive way. Rather than showing affectionate, chic couples in their advertising, Häagen-Dazs now presented time and genuine connection as the real scarce goods. Millennials loved the message and tests showed older adults would not leave the brand. Still, this message had an emotional tone and was difficult to deliver at the moment of purchase in a retail context where only price-offs, calories and new flavours seem to be critical shopper decision aspects. Therefore, Häagen-Dazs shifted to digital activations. In one case, Häagen-Dazs partnered with Secret Cinema to promote watching movies at home. Weekly newsletters recommended recipe combinations and included weekly codes to order the Häagen-Dazs flavour of the week delivered by Amazon.

FIVE WAYS TO SEE IF
INITIATIVE IS INCREMENTAL

1 Is total population (in country / region / catchment area) growing?

2 Is the product consumed by a target group that increases in size?

NEW CONSUMERS

3 Does the product appeal to a new target group that previously did not consume the category?

NEW TO THE CATEGORY

4 Is the product consumed at a higher frequency: more occasions, more times of the day?

HIGHER FREQUENCY

5 Do people like to consume more on current occasions?

HIGHER VOLUME

FURTHER QUESTIONS FOR HYPOTHESES ON SOURCE OF GROWTH:
- Did consumers previously consume your brand or a competitor brand?
- Did consumers previously consume another category?
- Did people previously consume something unregistered in retail or household panel data (e.g. products from kitchen garden, farmer's market, restaurant)?
- Is your initiative a triple win: for the supplier, the retailer and the consumer?

TOOL

2

How to identify the source of incrementality

User Group:	**R & S**
Challenge Level:	***
Time in Action Phase:	**3 h**

Situation

You want to understand whether your initiatives are actually contributing to further developing the category. Innovation is relevant for the retailer if the initiative is incremental to the category. Therefore, category initiatives such as product launches need to be checked for effects on the volume of category consumption.

Goal

Perform a critical self-assessment on whether the initiative you work on truly leads to category growth.

Preparation

- To track consumption behaviour in the past, you will need accessibility to data from loyalty card programmes, consumer panels or consumer diaries.

Action

- During this self-assessment, you explore five ways to see if your category initiative is incremental. See the five corresponding questions in the model. Be realistic and critical about whether your initiative truly adds volume to the category.
  - List the facts that support each of your answers.
  - Get clarity on the assumptions that you make.
  - Prepare a list of missing data to answer all questions.
- Optionally, decide at the end of the exercise if you need more fact-based evidence on the source of growth through some more detailed questions in the model.

Outcome

A ranking of category incrementality of initiatives with a list of arguments, assumptions and research questions per initiative.

Case in point #1: Incrementality in the core product

Domino's Pizza has always been an innovator in their category. Though they introduced new flavours on a continuous basis, they observed that most had short lives and delivered little growth. So they zoomed in on the core product, and noticed complaints about product quality (the most heard feedback was that the crust tasted like cardboard). They realised growth had to be achieved by delivering core products of better quality. To maximise insight gathering, they launched focus groups and a media campaign 'What is wrong with Domino's Pizza?' Sheets of paper with customer feedback were stuck in the corporate innovation kitchens. The Domino's Pizza chefs used the feedback and completely redesigned the recipe from scratch. And then, consumers who had participated in the focus groups received a surprise visit from the chefs so that they could taste the new pizza with a buttery crust, spicier sauce and tastier cheese. These efforts drove new, incremental sales of their core product.

Case in point #2: Real growth is based on volume metrics, not monetary metrics

Growing the dry pasta category is a challenge in many Western countries. For a long time, suppliers aimed to grow purchasing frequency through variation in new types of shapes and salsa. Incremental sales in value remained low as pasta had become a commodity that was typically stocked up on during promotions. The wide availability of value and private label products led to a lower average category price. Thus, brands started investigating the barriers to consumption. Many consumers leave the mostly wheat-based pasta category out of fear of gaining weight and concerns about carbohydrates. In response, suppliers such as Barilla have launched plant-based alternatives that contribute to green and healthier meals. These are gluten-free and high in fibre and proteins, such as red-lentil penne and chickpea rotini. Apart from product ingredients, new propositions that generate incremental sales in the category could also emerge from exploring product methods (e.g. organic), merchandising (e.g. fresh pasta in grocery cooler) and technology (e.g. 3D pasta printed for kids).

COSTS VERSUS ENJOYMENT

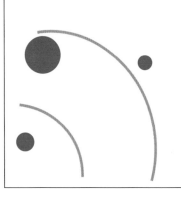

Saves the consumer costs;
Makes life easier;
Improves efficiency

Creates fun for consumer;
Makes you see new applications and benefits;
Enjoy using it

IDEA FUNNEL

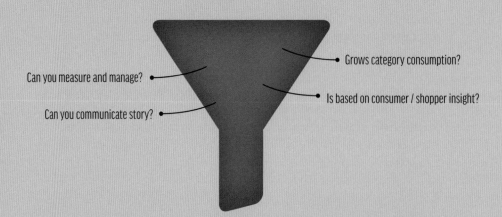

Grows category consumption?

Can you measure and manage?

Is based on consumer / shopper insight?

Can you communicate story?

TOOL

3

How to select the best category initiatives

User Group:	R & S
Challenge Level:	***
Time in Action Phase:	4 h

Situation

You want to prioritise initiatives according to consumer drivers in order to commit resources to the most promising ones. From a consumer perspective, this may happen according to the two ways they derive value: from cost reduction and/or from a more satisfying experience. The first will drive users into the category; the latter is important to keep shoppers engaged in the category. Often incremental category sales are included in this approach as a value indicator.

Goal

Identify the most promising ideas from a consumer perspective.

Preparation

- Describe your category initiative on a card, preferably with an image. Think of: promotions that attract new users to the category, new products with unique benefits, a shopper marketing campaign that excites shoppers.
- Prepare a flipchart for mapping the Costs versus Enjoyment; draw the axes as shown. Next, draw the Idea Funnel.
- Define criteria for the Idea Funnel (see four examples) and write your four questions on another flipchart sheet.

Action

- In a joint meeting with supplier and retailer teams, assess which category initiatives are driving Cost Improvement (vertical axis), Shopper Enjoyment (horizontal axis) and (Incremental) Sales of the initiative (size of the bubble). Score the first two elements on a range of one to ten, and estimate the latter in an absolute amount of revenue. For each card, draw a bubble on the flipchart, placing the name of the initiative next to the bubble for overview.
- Decide which initiatives are worth pursuing.
- Next, review the selected category initiatives with help of the Idea Funnel. Answer the four questions for each initiative card. Only if the initiative collects a yes to all questions do they drop through the funnel, ready for implementation.

Outcome

A selection of promising ideas that grow the category and are aligned between retailer and supplier.

Case in point #1: Revisiting category criteria, not just based on supplier segmentation

Historically many dairy companies were founded by the farmers themselves. Today, four of the top ten global dairy companies are still cooperatives. This creates an implicit pressure on the brand and shopper marketing teams to work only on dairy-based product ideas, since that is the way the industry is grouped. However, as consumer needs and expectations evolve, this way of categorising is in contrast with the growing demand for plant-based milks that are better for our planet. To future-proof the category, supplier teams start by defining the shopper needs from a broad perspective while ensuring that their analysis includes all sorts of solutions and substitutes, including non-dairy based. Even when this means extending into product types that leading brands don't manufacture themselves, communicating clearly on the category definition to their trade partners is essential for prioritisation of retail and merchandising strategies and thus beneficial to the suppliers too.

Case in point #2: Turn your customers into your advisors

Apparel company American Eagle has set up an advisory board, called AExME, in which teens advise them on all kind of business matters from product creation to selection of charities. Despite their young age, the teens have launched movements of their own to create a better and more inclusive society. One of their ideas was to develop a collection of apparel and accessories that donates 100% of proceeds to a charity (Delivering Good). Each item includes a label with a QR code that links to the charity's donation page, which helps sharing with others when wearing American Eagle clothes.

REVISED CATEGORY

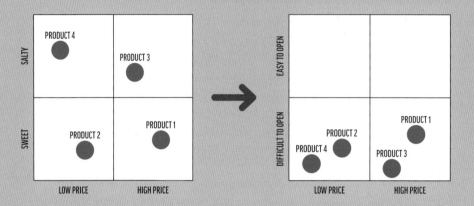

ATTRIBUTES FOR THE REVISED AXIS

Design	How would Apple design the product?
Aesthetics	How would Sephora create product appeal?
Efficiency	How would IKEA streamline the experience?
Corporate Citizen	How would Lush create value?
Emotion	How would Coca-Cola create the experience?
Data	How would Amazon improve the experience?

TOOL

How to scope for innovation

User Group:	R & S
Challenge Level:	****
Time in Action Phase:	2 h

Situation

You are looking for innovative ways to engage your shoppers. Even in the most static categories, shoppers are eager to try out new products for reasons that feel relevant to them. The challenge is to find an attribute that shoppers perceive as distinct and relevant and create a new way to group products that currently exist in the market.

Goal

To imagine new space for the category by assessing the relevance of a new attribute in the category

Preparation

- Suppliers and retailers often apply standard templates to categorise differences among products. In the preparation phase, gather information on how your organisation currently compares products: Which attributes are currently considered good indicators of preference?
- Gather a multifunctional team of four to six people.

Action

- In the first round, start playing with attributes from your list and see if you come up with a different way to segment the market.
- In the second round, take cues from the list of attributes as shown in the model, by asking the prompted questions or a variation of them.
- Place products in the new quadrant plot. Explore if a quadrant is an interesting and differential 'white space' where no product is currently active.

Outcome

Identification of revised attributes and new, differential white spaces in the category where innovation is possible.

Case in point #1: Predict the product winners of tomorrow

The German drugstore Rossmann has improved the predictions of product launch success (brand) by addressing the increasing versatility and fickleness of shopper behaviour (shopper) with the help of artificial intelligence (technology) taking into account privacy concerns (society). Rossmann uses search behaviour on Google, Amazon and other sources to visualise trends for the next one and a half years and to forecast the impact in their (online) stores. Rossmann knows which colours, ingredients and products will become popular six months or more in advance. This has improved the efficiency of product launches and has created higher shopper satisfaction.

Case in point #2: Constantly on the lookout for new ways to segment the market

Even a mundane category such as shampoo keeps on changing as a result of a battle among global brands and the consequent influx of new products. The game revolves around identifying a new aspect that influences the way shoppers make decisions on their shampoo purchases. A great example is when P&G invented the 2-in-1 shampoo that combines the benefit of shampoo (cleaning) and conditioner (managing your hair and giving it shine). From that moment on, P&G could set all products of the competition aside as non-2-in-1s and present theirs as a category growth opportunity. Fortunately for the other A-brands, the shampoo category offers many ways of looking at and segmenting the market in a fresh way. To name a few: target group (e.g. kids), benefit (e.g. anti-dandruff), ingredients (e.g. herbal), price (e.g. value brand), channel (e.g. hair salons), type of hair (e.g. oily or dyed hair) and packaging (e.g. large size), which means that there is always space to be made for innovative products.

THE S.M.A.R.T. MODEL
FOR SMALL BASKETS

S — SOCIO-DEMO

Often consumer panel & loyalty card data are underrepresented in small baskets, be sure to ask the usual socio-demo.

M — MOOD

Discover through smileys in which mood-state shoppers are: Delighted, In a hurry?

A — AFFINITY

Which other items did shoppers buy? Are these accidental, or in which way are they associated?

R — REASON

Why did people buy the category? How would they describe their shopping mission?

T — TYPE

Which type of product did they buy? Why this flavour? What would they do if it had been out-of-stock?

TOOL

5

How to boost the value of a small basket

User Group:	R & S
Challenge Level:	****
Time in Action Phase:	1 d

Situation

You wonder whether there are untapped opportunities in small baskets. We might underappreciate incidental purchases, accidental shoppers and small baskets, while in combination they drive store traffic and category unit rotation. Also, it is not reviewed often, as data from consumer panels and loyalty cards may not cover small baskets well as shoppers do not make the effort to register the transaction.

Goal

Increase category sales by driving small baskets.

Preparation

- Define a small basket, for example a one item basket or any basket below €5.
- Through transaction data, find out at which moment small basket trips for your category are made.
- Gather a team of ten people.
- Select ten different stores that will be visited at relevant but different moments.

Action

- Observe at checkout when a shopper makes a small basket purchase. Ask the shopper for a couple minutes to do a short survey.
- Ask S.M.A.R.T. questions from the model provided and any open-ended questions if there is time left or when the purchase includes an item of interest to your research.
- Combine the answers with any observations made. What did you learn on the buying motivations and behaviour of small basket shoppers?
- Try to apply the learnings to your own category: Do you need to relocate the category, do you have ideas for cross-selling, etc.?

Outcome

Concrete action points and inspiration for driving more sales from small baskets.

Case in point #1: Complement with data at moment of purchase

Some small shopping baskets get overlooked easily because most research methods do not capture their sales well (coverage rate is low). For example, registration through consumer household panels requires the scanning of products at home; however, children are likely to consume the energy drinks and bags of crisps before they are scanned. The closer you get to the moment of purchase, the more reliable the data is. Suppliers that operate in impulse and personal-use categories actually capture sales by scanning of receipts with smartphones. The trick is to triangulate sources of data, such as shopper intercepts, market research and surveys to check for consistency in the patterns and to complement the data from different angles.

Case in point #2: Drive sales through digital channels

Alibaba's Hema stores combine the roles of grocery supermarket, restaurant and distribution centre for online orders. People visit Hema for the quality and affordable pricing of fresh products, especially fish products. These also happen to be categories that are more delicate for home deliveries, even if they only take a maximum of thirty minutes as in Hema's case. A user-friendly app encourages shoppers to order most of their grocery list for home delivery in the Hema app. As a result, about half of the floor space is allocated to non-selling activities (space for logistics, personnel, storage, etc). The other half is dedicated to on premises sales, causing in-store assortment to remain small due to the availability of space. Shoppers are directed to the online environment by encouraging the use of smartphones and digital devices. The Hema concept has the rare mission to keep the number of products sold in-store low, while at the same time excelling in experience delivery (e.g. in-store cooking and dining), freshness (e.g. focus on seafood) and speed of shopping (e.g. fast payments through facial recognition, AI-enabled personal product suggestions, scan & go with QR codes).

EXCITING TECHNOLOGIES

Artificial Intelligence

3D Printing

SOCIETAL CHALLENGES

Urbanisation

Energy

BRAND INITIATIVES

New Flavour

Game on Social Media

SHOPPER EMOTIONS

Choice Stress

Energy

TECH

SOCIETY

BRAND

EMOTION

TOOL

6

How to bundle new brand ideas into category themes

User Group:	S
Challenge Level:	***
Time in Action Phase:	4 h

Situation

You wish to present your marketing department's brand initiatives to the retailer in a convincing and inspiring way. Ideally, you leverage the category drivers that support the category vision. Or, if these are not available, you need to find other ways to bundle the brand initiatives that inspire retailers to drive innovation and activation. Your aim is to create a category story with relevant brand activation.

Goal

Connecting trends that stimulate category growth with initiatives for brands developed by the marketing team.

Preparation

- Ask six to eight participants from various functions to create a list of themes in four areas: exciting technologies, challenges in society, shopper emotions and brand initiatives.
- Print these on single cards and sort the cards into four stacks of themes.
- Prepare large A2-sized pieces of paper.

Action

- Work in groups of three or four.
- Pick a card from each of the four stacks.
- Brainstorm how you can connect the themes from the four cards. When you find an interesting connection, place them on the table in the middle of the large piece of paper. Write down ideas around them. This could look like a mind map whereby you explore different creative paths.
- Complete the exercise within six minutes and start another one.
- Collect ideas and solutions per brand initiative from mind maps.

Outcome

Building blocks to create relevance in your story on how new ideas and solutions drive the category plan from a supplier brand perspective.

Case in point #1: Look around for themes presented by partners

Made.com was not the first furniture and home decoration brand that gave people the chance of winning a home makeover. However, they did so in a creative way under the platform of a partner.

Made.com embraced the opportunity when Amsterdam's Schiphol Airport invited them to create a homely feeling for their passengers at the gates. While waiting for their flight, passengers could relax in the comfortably designed living rooms. For the airport, this was a great way to differentiate themselves and to conduct experiments that encouraged passengers to shop at the gate and order online. Made.com had good results from the promotion. It was a great way for passengers to try new sofas and even order them online while they waited for their flight to depart, which could otherwise feel like wasted time.

Case in point #2: Find out what is really important in the target groups' lives

Shoppers are increasingly aware of the importance of maintaining health through prevention and supplementation, yet may easily oversee the addition of a new product line, like chewable Centrum supplements. There is an abundance of supplement products and price-off promotions in supermarkets shouting for attention. There is also the fact that this target group have busy lifestyles. Centrum decided to leverage the latter in their communication. A personal trainer named Tiny Trainer that fits into bathrooms and medicine cabinets represents the positive reinforcement and encouragement that personal trainers give to physical activity, but in the context of health supplements. Tiny Trainer recognises today's hectic schedules but also addresses the importance of a healthy routine. In a playful way, she provides positive feedback, and hops on the trend of personal trainers with the purpose of instilling healthy habits in adults before their forties.

Concluding thought:
Be a great unlearner and relearner

New technologies allow retailers and suppliers to reach the same level of personalisation for shoppers as they experience in mom-and-pop stores. However, it is not just a matter of investments in data availability, analytical software and smart technology that make categories and retail models future-proof. First of all, technology serves a mission: to make the shopping experience more enjoyable and more relevant. Also, getting it to work requires vision from the senior management, new skills from the retailer and supplier teams and increasingly the strengthening of partnerships across the value chain. All these aspects come together in the category management concept and thus, it offers a great platform for future growth – of both your business and team work. The framework from some 25 years ago needs an update though. By combining this concept with ideas from the fields of Customer Experience, Product Innovation and Design Thinking, we developed new techniques to grow the category, satisfy shopper needs and work together with trade partners.

This book could be seen as a store where you wander from department to department, and shop for what is required for the mission you are on. Like in a real store, your mission is highly context dependent. We started with the category strategy and discussed important concepts such as the definition of the category with the consumption needs as the starting point, and category roles for the allocation of investments. Next, because retail brands have grown stronger, we need to know in which direction the retailer wishes to take the category. This retail strategy comes alive when discussing fresh ways of analysing assortment, pricing and promotion. Digitisation accelerates the integration of retail and supplier organisations and therefore finding and building the right partnerships is an essential organisational capability. Too often it stops here, but in my experience thinking about the service level of the product opens new ways to differentiate your brand. Finally, innovation of your category and your way of working is needed to keep the category healthy.

It seems only natural that the moments of learning come early in our lives and our careers. With the speed of society we need to learn all kinds of new things ever more quickly, and also when we grow older. Still, the most formative and decisive moments seem to happen in those moments when we unlearn and relearn things. And I find that un- and relearning are more difficult than learning, but as important to grow as a professional. We need to let go of old habits, assumptions and thinking models:

- From dividing people into shopper segments to building personal relationships with memorable experiences.
- From defining rules of the game in a top-down manner to creating shopping contexts where shoppers engage and co-create.
- From perfect planning and rules of the game to entrepreneurial team spirit.
- From pulling transactions through linear distribution channels to exploring networks of partnerships.

When I reflect on the times I unlearnt and relearnt something, I would describe the circumstances as follows: I was honest with myself when my first approach had failed, there was a great mentor around, I had stepped into a new world, and, most importantly, I had tried something. To be a great unlearner does not mean to me that you throw away everything you have learnt – certainly not! My hope is that this book will provide inspiration for your thinking, that you start playing around with help of the tools in the book, that you evaluate what works for you in your situation and share your learnings with others. Enjoy!

About the author

Constant Berkhout is a passionate practitioner of retail marketing and shopper insights. He obtained a Master of Science in Economics Cum Laude with a major in Marketing at the University of Groningen in the Netherlands. His curiosity and career took him across the world to live in Argentina, Belgium, the UK and the USA. Constant is also the author of *Retail Marketing Strategy: Delivering Shopper Delight* (2016) and *Assortment and Merchandising Strategy: Building a Retail Plan to Improve Shopper Experience* (2019).

Through his own agency, Constant works with retailers and suppliers in Europe, the Middle East and Asia including Conagra Brands, Danone, GrandVision, Heineken, JDE, Jumbo, Migros, SPAR International, Sonos, and Xenos. Most of the assignments focus on retail format development, category management strategy, data analytics and shopper marketing. Before setting up his own agency, he gained broad experience across a large number of categories, functional areas, and countries:

- At retailers De Boer Winkelbedrijven and Ahold Delhaize, Constant got acquainted with the principles of retail and category management.
- For Kraft Foods, Constant set up their trade marketing practice and worked as customer manager to large supermarket chains.
- At Gillette/Procter & Gamble, he led business restructuring in commercial and value-chain departments in several European countries. Later he was given overall responsibility for the marketing at the business-to-business division in Europe.
- At PepsiCo, he first assumed responsibility for consumer insights and innovation for Northern Europe. In his last role at PepsiCo, he was responsible for shopper insights and marketing in more than 45 countries in Europe. He set up trade marketing in Eastern European countries such as Russia. For Western European markets, he increased customer intimacy with customers such as Carrefour, Casino and Tesco. He worked closely with colleagues in North America to apply breakthrough technologies in the areas of neuro-research and data analytics.

Constant is married, and he and his wife have two children. In his free time, he loves reading and travelling, and although he was a passionate handball player in the past, most time on the sports field is now spent watching his children play soccer and basketball.

Endorsements

'A great read for both retail and A-brand players that are serious about a consistent approach to shopper-centric category thinking. Following this toolkit will deliver a clear category vision and strategy that will optimise execution in store and on shelf. Once the category work has been done, yearly updates will be easy to fine-tune based on new shopper and category insights.'

Wim Destoop, VP General Manager North West Europe, PepsiCo

'Constant's experience and passion always centre around category management, the place where retailers and suppliers, consumers and shoppers, and brands and private labels meet. He has funnelled this expertise and passion into this highly practical book, which is useful for anyone active in the retail space, from novice to experienced professional. This toolkit – which is spiced up with a range of illustrations – can be read from beginning to end in one go, though it can also be picked up regularly when faced with a specific challenge. It will help the reader with ideas and a concrete plan. I would highly recommend this book!

Jeroen Van de Broek, Managing Director Belgium, FrieslandCampina

'A great reference book for everyone involved in the category management process, from junior up to C-level. The book is very practical, to the point and easy to read.'

Wouter Lefevere, Managing Director
Category Management Nederland, ALDI

'How wonderful it is to unlearn and learn anew! And for most of us this is not a choice, as consumers across the world adapt to changing lifestyles and new channels. Constant Berkhout's book is just that! A compact, wholesome toolkit to assess and reassess the way we look at categories and how to build brands with them: from setting broader goals to actioning the details. This toolkit has everything you will need to form a holistic approach towards category management – both for now and the foreseeable future. Happy Unlearning!'

Pearlraj Cannivady, VP Marketing &
Omnichannel, SPAR Hypermarkets India

'It is important for Shopping Insights people to understand how to make the buying process easy, painless and pleasant for shoppers. To do so, you need to get under the skin of the shoppers and to step into the shoes of the retailers. This book helps you to understand how to help retailers to help shoppers shop, which will result in category growth. The approach of an holistic toolkit is brilliant: the 42 tools are practical, actionable, well explained and run through collaborative exercises, inspiring stories and useful suggestions.'

Iris Cremers, Global Shopping Insight Manager, Unilever

'This is an engaging and outstanding book for anyone who wants to apply innovative category management methods to win the heart of the shopper. The Retail Innovation Toolkit provides inspiring case studies and fun exercises that encourage teams to build category strategies that are strong, creative and refreshing.'

Jacques Hayaux du Tilly, Group Assortment & Supply Chain Director, Maxeda DIY Group

'The Retail Innovation Toolkit is theoretically underpinned but above all pragmatic, high level, and accessible, with striking examples! A must for anyone who wants to achieve more in the dynamic world of FMCG, either as a retailer or on the manufacturers' side. Really good!'

Rob Mienis, Trade Marketing Manager Retail, Van Geloven

'An accessible, practical book full of ideas, helpful guidelines, and exercises to work through together for category growth.'

Linda van Rijn, Product Director UI/ Client Platforms & Core Analytics Tools, Global Product Management, GfK

'The new retail landscape requires completely different category management. Despite the globalised supply chain, consumer needs have never been more local and individual. Fortunately, data enable to align the relationships between supplier, retailer and consumer better than ever. Berkhout's Toolkit is the perfect companion, packed with very practical and hands-on exercises, not from an ivory tower but straight from the field.'

Jorg Snoeck, founder of RetailDetail and co-author of *The Future of Shopping*